40 Days with Jesus

A STUDY ON THE
LIFE OF CHRIST

THE DAILY GRACE CO.®

Study Suggestions

We believe that the Bible is true, trustworthy, and timeless and that it is vitally important for all believers. These study suggestions are intended to help you more effectively study Scripture as you seek to know and love God through His Word.

SUGGESTED STUDY TOOLS

- A Bible

- A double-spaced, printed copy of the Scripture passages that this study covers. You can use a website like *www.biblegateway.com* to copy the text of a passage and print out a double-spaced copy to be able to mark on easily

- A journal to write notes or prayers

- Pens, colored pencils, and highlighters

- A dictionary to look up unfamiliar words

HOW TO USE THIS STUDY

Begin your study time in prayer. Ask God to reveal Himself to you, to help you understand what you are reading, and to transform you with His Word (Psalm 119:18).

Before you read what is written in each day of the study itself, read the assigned passages of Scripture for that day. Use your double-spaced copy to circle, underline, highlight, draw arrows, and mark in any way you would like to help you dig deeper as you work through a passage.

Read the daily written content provided for the current study day.

Answer the questions that appear at the end of each study day.

HOW TO STUDY THE BIBLE

The inductive method provides tools for deeper and more intentional Bible study. To study the Bible inductively, work through the steps below after reading background information on the book.

1 OBSERVATION & COMPREHENSION
Key question: What does the text say?

After reading the daily Scripture in its entirety at least once, begin working with smaller portions of the Scripture. Read a passage of Scripture repetitively, and then mark the following items in the text:

- Key or repeated words and ideas
- Key themes
- Transition words (Ex: therefore, but, because, if/then, likewise, etc.)
- Lists
- Comparisons & Contrasts
- Commands
- Unfamiliar words (look these up in a dictionary)
- Questions you have about the text

2 INTERPRETATION
Key question: What does the text mean?

Once you have annotated the text, work through the following steps to help you interpret its meaning:

- Read the passage in other versions for a better understanding of the text.
- Read cross-references to help interpret Scripture with Scripture.
- Paraphrase or summarize the passage to check for understanding.
- Identify how the text reflects the metanarrative of Scripture, which is the story of creation, fall, redemption, and restoration.
- Read trustworthy commentaries if you need further insight into the meaning of the passage.

3 APPLICATION
Key Question: How should the truth of this passage change me?

Bible study is not merely an intellectual pursuit. The truths about God, ourselves, and the gospel that we discover in Scripture should produce transformation in our hearts and lives. Answer the following questions as you consider what you have learned in your study:

- What attributes of God's character are revealed in the passage?

    Consider places where the text directly states the character of God, as well as how His character is revealed through His words and actions.

- What do I learn about myself in light of who God is?

    Consider how you fall short of God's character, how the text reveals your sin nature, and what it says about your new identity in Christ.

- How should this truth change me?

    A passage of Scripture may contain direct commands telling us what to do or warnings about sins to avoid in order to help us grow in holiness. Other times our application flows out of seeing ourselves in light of God's character. As we pray and reflect on how God is calling us to change in light of His Word, we should be asking questions like, "How should I pray for God to change my heart?" and "What practical steps can I take toward cultivating habits of holiness?"

THE ATTRIBUTES OF GOD

ETERNAL

God has no beginning and no end. He always was, always is, and always will be.

HAB. 1:12 / REV. 1:8 / IS. 41:4

FAITHFUL

God is incapable of anything but fidelity. He is loyally devoted to His plan and purpose.

2 TIM. 2:13 / DEUT. 7:9
HEB. 10:23

GOOD

God is pure; there is no defilement in Him. He is unable to sin, and all He does is good.

GEN. 1:31 / PS. 34:8 / PS. 107:1

GRACIOUS

God is kind, giving us gifts and benefits we do not deserve.

2 KINGS 13:23 / PS. 145:8
IS. 30:18

HOLY

God is undefiled and unable to be in the presence of defilement. He is sacred and set-apart.

REV. 4:8 / LEV. 19:2 / HAB. 1:13

INCOMPREHENSIBLE & TRANSCENDENT

God is high above and beyond human understanding. He is unable to be fully known.

PS. 145:3 / IS. 55:8-9
ROM. 11:33-36

IMMUTABLE

God does not change. He is the same yesterday, today, and tomorrow.

1 SAM. 15:29 / ROM. 11:29
JAMES 1:17

INFINITE

God is limitless. He exhibits all of His attributes perfectly and boundlessly.

ROM. 11:33-36 / IS. 40:28
PS. 147:5

JEALOUS

God is desirous of receiving the praise and affection He rightly deserves.

EX. 20:5 / DEUT. 4:23-24
JOSH. 24:19

JUST

God governs in perfect justice. He acts in accordance with justice. In Him, there is no wrongdoing or dishonesty.

IS. 61:8 / DEUT. 32:4 / PS. 146:7-9

LOVING

God is eternally, enduringly, steadfastly loving and affectionate. He does not forsake or betray His covenant love.

JN. 3:16 / EPH. 2:4-5 / 1 JN. 4:16

MERCIFUL

God is compassionate, withholding from us the wrath that we deserve.

TITUS 3:5 / PS. 25:10
LAM. 3:22-23

OMNIPOTENT

God is all-powerful; His strength is unlimited.

MAT. 19:26 / JOB 42:1-2
JER. 32:27

OMNIPRESENT

God is everywhere; His presence is near and permeating.

PROV. 15:3 / PS. 139:7-10
JER. 23:23-24

OMNISCIENT

God is all-knowing; there is nothing unknown to Him.

PS. 147:4 / I JN. 3:20
HEB. 4:13

PATIENT

God is long-suffering and enduring. He gives ample opportunity for people to turn toward Him.

ROM. 2:4 / 2 PET. 3:9 / PS. 86:15

SELF-EXISTENT

God was not created but exists by His power alone.

PS. 90:1-2 / JN. 1:4 / JN. 5:26

SELF-SUFFICIENT

God has no needs and depends on nothing, but everything depends on God.

IS. 40:28-31 / ACTS 17:24-25
PHIL. 4:19

SOVEREIGN

God governs over all things; He is in complete control.

COL. 1:17 / PS. 24:1-2
1 CHRON. 29:11-12

TRUTHFUL

God is our measurement of what is fact. By Him are we able to discern true and false.

JN. 3:33 / ROM. 1:25 / JN. 14:6

WISE

God is infinitely knowledgeable and is judicious with His knowledge.

IS. 46:9-10 / IS. 55:9 / PROV. 3:19

WRATHFUL

God stands in opposition to all that is evil. He enacts judgment according to His holiness, righteousness, and justice.

PS. 69:24 / JN. 3:36 / ROM. 1:18

METANARRATIVE OF SCRIPTURE

Creation

In the beginning, God created the universe. He made the world and everything in it. He created humans in His own image to be His representatives on the earth.

Fall

The first humans, Adam and Eve, disobeyed God by eating from the fruit of the Tree of Knowledge of Good and Evil. Because of sin, the world was cursed. The punishment for sin is death, and because of Adam's original sin, all humans are sinful and condemned to death.

Redemption

God sent His Son to become a human and redeem His people. Jesus Christ lived a sinless life but died on the cross to pay the penalty for sin. He resurrected from the dead and ascended into heaven. All who put their faith in Jesus are saved from death and freely receive the gift of eternal life.

Restoration

One day, Jesus Christ will return again and restore all that sin destroyed. He will usher in a new heaven and new earth where all who trust in Him will live eternally with glorified bodies in the presence of God.

TABLE OF CONTENTS

HOW TO USE THIS STUDY FOR THE OBSERVATION OF LENT	12
PASSION WEEK TIMELINE	14
JESUS: OUR PROPHET, PRIEST, AND KING	18
DAY 1: JESUS'S BIRTH	21
DAY 2: JESUS PRESENTED IN THE TEMPLE	25
DAY 3: JESUS GROWING UP	29
DAY 4: DISCUSSING SCRIPTURE WITH SCHOLARS	33
REFLECTION	36
DAY 5: JESUS'S FAMILY AND BIRTHPLACE	39
DAY 6: JESUS'S BAPTISM	43
DAY 7: THE TEMPTATION OF JESUS	47
DAY 8: JESUS'S MINISTRY AND MESSAGE	51
DAY 9: JESUS THE ETERNAL WORD	55
DAY 10: TESTIMONY OF JOHN	59
REFLECTION	62
DAY 11: THE FIRST DISCIPLES	65
DAY 12: JESUS TURNS WATER TO WINE	69
DAY 13: BEATITUDES	73
DAY 14: THE LORD'S PRAYER	77
DAY 15: JESUS HEALS THE LEPER	81
DAY 16: THE COMING ONE	85
REFLECTION	88
DAY 17: JESUS CARRIES OUR BURDENS	91
DAY 18: THE PARABLE OF THE SOWER	95
DAY 19: UNBELIEF IN HIS HOMETOWN	99
DAY 20: JESUS AND NICODEMAS	103
DAY 21: JESUS AND THE WOMAN AT THE WELL	107
DAY 22: WALKING ON WATER	111
REFLECTION	114

DAY 23: THE FEEDING OF THE FIVE THOUSAND	117
DAY 24: BREAD OF LIFE	121
DAY 25: LIGHT OF THE WORLD	125
DAY 26: THE GOOD SHEPHERD	129
DAY 27: JESUS REVEALS HIMSELF	133
DAY 28: THE GOOD SAMARITAN	137
REFLECTION	140
DAY 29: THE TRANSFIGURATION	143
DAY 30: PARABLE OF THE PRODIGAL SON	147
DAY 31: RAISING OF LAZARUS	151
DAY 32: TRIUMPHANT ENTRY	155
DAY 33: JESUS ENTERS THE TEMPLE	159
DAY 34: LAST SUPPER	163
REFLECTION	166
DAY 35: JESUS WASHES THE DISCIPLES FEET	169
DAY 36: JESUS THE WAY, THE TRUTH, AND THE LIFE	173
DAY 37: JESUS THE TRUE VINE	179
DAY 38: JESUS'S HIGH PRIESTLY PRAYER	183
DAY 39: ARREST AT GETHSEMANE	187
DAY 40: CRUCIFIXION AND BURIAL	191
DAY 41: RESURRECTION AND ASCENSION	195
THE NUMBER 40: THEMES IN SCRIPTURE	198
MESSIANIC PROPHECIES OF THE OLD TESTAMENT FULFILLED IN CHRIST	199
WHAT IS THE GOSPEL?	202

How to Use this Study

FOR THE OBSERVATION OF LENT

The Christian church started the season of Lent as a way to prepare one's heart for Easter. Originally, Lent began on a Sunday and lasted until Maundy Thursday—the Thursday before Easter—so it was exactly 40 days in length. However, since Sundays were Sabbath days and considered days of rest, Lent was eventually extended so that there were a total of 40 days devoted to fasting that excluded those days of rest, and that is how *40 Days with Jesus* is designed. If used in conjunction with Lent, it begins on Ash Wednesday and finishes on Easter Sunday.

In addition to the length of Lent changing, the structure has also varied through the years. In the past, the forty days of Lent involved prayer and fasting from a particular food. The idea behind this fasting is to reflect the forty days of fasting Jesus did in the wilderness before beginning His ministry. In our current day and age, what people choose to give up during Lent is their own choice. Some give up a type of food, while others give up a tangible item or form of technology. The choice to give something up reflects a desire to make a form of sacrifice. Like sacrificing a type of food, we give up something that we often rely on so we can rely wholeheartedly on the Lord. When we feel pulled toward what we have given up, we are reminded to depend on the Lord above all things. We must not see whatever sacrifice we make during Lent as the means to earn salvation with God. Rather, sacrifices during Lent are a response to the salvation we have received through Christ. As we sacrifice something of our own, we are reminded of the sacrifice Jesus made for our sake. Even if you do not choose to give something up, Lent is still a special time of personal reflection.

40 Days with Jesus can be used as a companion to help prepare your heart for Easter, though it may certainly be used any time of year. If you decide to follow the study for Lent, the first week of the study allows you to begin on Ash Wednesday, and the last week of the study enables you to finish on Easter Sunday, so there are a total of 41 "study days." You may decide to combine the last two days so that you finish everything the Saturday before Easter.

Through daily Scripture readings, you will have the opportunity to feast upon the Word of God, regardless of when you choose to work through the following pages. As you do, you will learn that daily time with the Lord and in His Word is what gives us true satisfaction and life. By spending 40 days with Jesus, you will learn to feast on the Bread of Life, Jesus Christ. May this study encourage your heart as you prepare for Easter and cause you to treasure the gospel more deeply.

40 DAYS WITH JESUS - LENT SCHEDULE

CALENDAR DAY	DAY	CALENDAR DAY	DAY	CALENDAR DAY	DAY
ASH WEDNESDAY	1	MONDAY	17	MONDAY	29
THURSDAY	2	TUESDAY	18	TUESDAY	30
FRIDAY	3	WEDNESDAY	19	WEDNESDAY	31
SATURDAY	4	THURSDAY	20	THURSDAY	32
SUNDAY	R*	FRIDAY	21	FRIDAY	33
MONDAY	5	SATURDAY	22	SATURDAY	34
TUESDAY	6	SUNDAY	R	SUNDAY	R
WEDNESDAY	7	MONDAY	23	MONDAY	35
THURSDAY	8	TUESDAY	24	TUESDAY	36
FRIDAY	9	WEDNESDAY	25	WEDNESDAY	37
SATURDAY	10	THURSDAY	26	THURSDAY	38
SUNDAY	R	FRIDAY	27	FRIDAY	39
MONDAY	11	SATURDAY	28	SATURDAY	40
TUESDAY	12	SUNDAY	R	EASTER SUNDAY	41
WEDNESDAY	13				
THURSDAY	14				
FRIDAY	15				
SATURDAY	16				
SUNDAY	R				

R* *Reflection days may be combined with the previous day or completed on Sundays.*

Passion Week Timeline

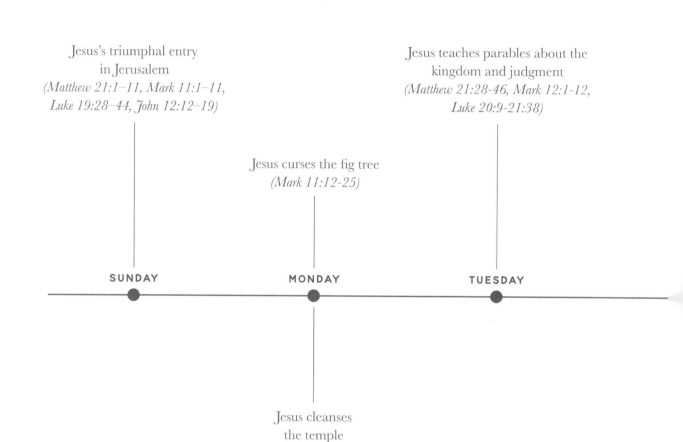

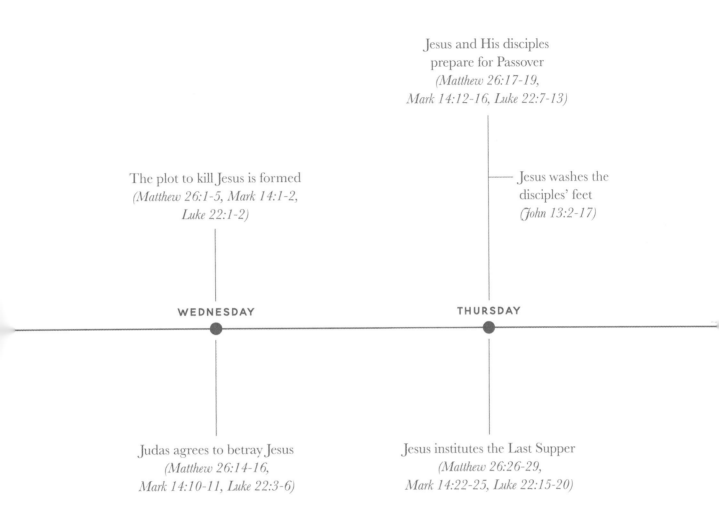

Passion Week Timeline / 15

PASSION WEEK TIMELINE, CONT.

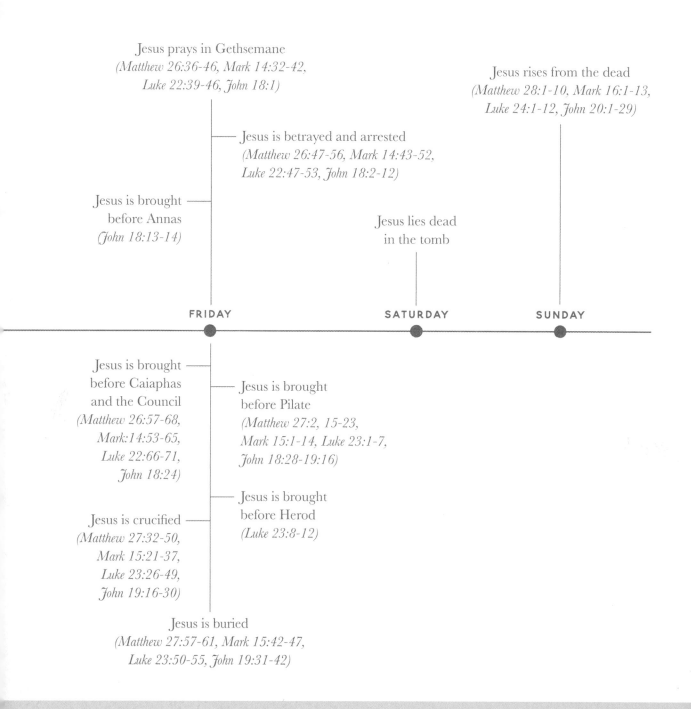

PASSION WEEK LOCATIONS

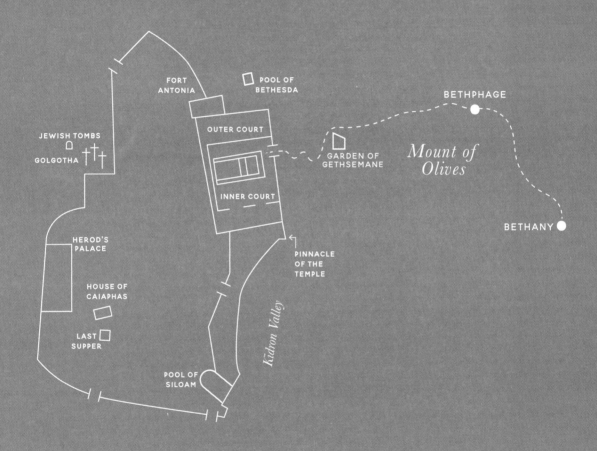

Jesus,

OUR PROPHET, PRIEST, AND KING

PROPHET

God used prophets to proclaim the Word of God. Out of all the prophets in Scripture, Jesus is the greatest. What makes Jesus a great prophet is not that He speaks the words of God but that He is the Word of God. John 1:1 says, "In the beginning was the Word, and the Word was with God, and the Word was God." Just as a prophet has the authority to speak God's words, Jesus's authority from His deity and relationship with the Father authenticates His teachings. Because He is God and comes from God, all of His words are true. Like prophets in the Old Testament who warned people of judgment and called them to repentance, Jesus's words and teachings throughout His ministry proclaimed God's judgment but also His salvation.

PRIEST

In the Old Testament, priests were responsible for performing sacrifices on behalf of the people to atone for their sins. In these sacrifices, the priests acted as intercessors by coming to the Lord on behalf of the people to ask for forgiveness. Christ is not just a priest. He is the Great High Priest. By His sacrifice on the cross, He provided atonement for our sins. Unlike the priests who have to continue their sacrifices for people's salvation, Jesus's sacrifice is once and for all because He is perfect. His atonement brings about reconciliation between man and God by the covering of their sins. Jesus also provides perfect intercession between God and man. Those who come to faith in Christ receive Jesus as a permanent intercessor. Hebrews 7:25 says, "Therefore, He is able to save completely those who come to God through him, since he always lives to intercede for them." By His sacrifice and intercession, Jesus is our mediator. He acted on our behalf through His sacrifices and continues to act on our behalf by bringing our needs to God. Because of Him, we have access to God forever.

KING

All the kings of the Old Testament pale in comparison to King Jesus. The greatest of kings was said to be King David, but it is through David's line that the true King comes. Jesus is the King of kings and the Lord of lords. Unlike the kings of the Old Testament who failed to obey the Lord, Jesus is perfectly obedient to the Lord. He is not a king who rules unjustly, for He executes perfect justice and righteousness. Christ's kingship also attests to His great rule and reign over all things. He is sovereign over the whole world. Jesus is the King who ushers in the kingdom of God and invites people to join His kingdom. By His great power, He has conquered sin and death and will one day remove it forever. The Lordship of Christ is worthy of our glory and praise.

What makes Jesus a great prophet is not that He speaks the words of God but that He is the Word of God.

He is the Great High Priest. By His sacrifice on the cross, He provided atonement for our sins.

He is not a king who rules unjustly, for He executes perfect justice and righteousness.

DAY 1

"HIS RULE AND REIGN WOULD BRING PEACE TO ALL PEOPLE.

Jesus's Birth

READ LUKE 2:1-20

A man ties his sandals and saddles his donkey. He places his pregnant wife on the donkey, and they journey toward Bethlehem. It was time for them to register in the census, and although they lived in Nazareth, the man was from David's lineage, which meant he must register in the city of David, Bethlehem. In the city, his wife tells him the baby is coming. Due to the census, too many people were crowding the city, so they could not find a place to stay. Instead, the man and woman find a stable, and the baby is born.

At first glance, this story seems like any other. If we open this passage up with no context, it would appear fairly normal, even though birth in a stable is unusual. But as the text continues to unfold, it is clear that this is no ordinary story and no ordinary baby.

We move from this account to a different perspective happening in the shepherd fields. As the shepherds are tending to their flock, an angel appears to them. The glory of the Lord shone around the angel, causing the shepherds to cower in response. But the angel says not to be afraid, as his message is not of condemnation but comfort. The angel reveals how he came to share "good news of great joy" (Luke 2:10). The term "good news" means "gospel," and this is the first occurrence of the gospel in Luke's story. The gospel message of the baby's birth would bring joy to all people. For the Jewish people have been waiting for deliverance from the Law for hundreds of years. They longed for the Savior who would come so that there would be another way, for their sacrifices given according to the Law could never fully atone for their sins. Only the Messiah for whom they longed could bring grace and freedom and life everlasting. The promised Deliverer—who was prophesied about in the Old Testament—is here, and joy has come.

The angel further reveals the baby's identity when he gives Him three names: Savior, Messiah, and Lord. "Savior" means "deliverer," and "Messiah" is another word for "Christ." "Lord" is used in reference to the name "Yahweh" and is the divine name of God. These three titles identify that this baby is more than a mere child; He is God in the flesh.

This announcement is followed by a multitude of angels singing praises to God. This gospel message is one of astounding glory, both attesting to the glory of God in heaven and the glory of God here on earth. The angels also pair God's glory with peace on earth. This child is the promised Savior and Messiah. His rule and reign would bring peace to all people who belong to Him. But this peace would be different than what the people had in mind. Their focus is on the peace that would come from peaceful lives free from Roman oppression. But this Savior would do more than fix the brokenness of society; He would fix the brokenness between God and man, restoring the peaceful relationship God once had with man before the Fall (Genesis 3).

This text does not reveal how Christ would bring about this peace, but it whispers of what is to come. Luke speaks to the fulfillment of Christ in the Old Testament through subtle hints in the text. One is the location of the birth of this child and his lineage. Luke 2:4 reveals that Joseph is not only traveling to the city of David; his lineage belongs to David. And in Luke 2:11, the angels announce that the birth of Jesus has taken place in the city of David. This fulfills the prophecy of the location of the Promised One's birth being in Bethlehem in Micah 5:2 and fulfills the prophecy of the lineage of Christ in Jeremiah 23:5-6. Luke also speaks of Christ's humility. The place of Christ's birth is no accident. This great Deliverer was born in a stable and placed in a manger. While it may seem like a contradiction that the One who angels praised gloriously would be placed in a manger, this detail foreshadows Christ's humble and lowly status. His humble birth is only the beginning of a life of humiliation. This baby would grow up to be a man who would bring deliverance from sin by dying on a cross. He would rise from the grave, triumphing over sin and death, and those who believed in Him would have everlasting peace and joy.

The text ends with the shepherds glorifying and praising God after seeing the baby promised by the angels. But Mary's response is different; she is treasuring and meditating on the promises for her child in her heart. As we begin our journey of studying the life of Jesus, our responses should be like those of the shepherds and Mary. The message of the gospel propels us toward glorification and contemplation. God is worthy of praise for sending His Son to earth to die for our sins. The goodness of the gospel is something we should treasure and meditate on every day of our lives. Let us be filled with awe and wonder over the greatness of Jesus and treasure the truth of the gospel in our hearts.

> **THE GOSPEL MESSAGE OF THE BABY'S BIRTH WOULD BRING JOY TO ALL PEOPLE.**

day one questions

How does this passage speak to the faithfulness of the Lord?

Why does God choose shepherds to be the first people to hear about Jesus?

Is your response to the gospel one of praise and contemplation? Spend some time praising God for who He is and meditating on the truth of the gospel.

DAY 2

> WHEN HE COMES AGAIN, JESUS WILL BRING ULTIMATE JOY TO OUR SOULS.

Jesus Presented in the Temple

READ LUKE 2:22-38

Mary and Joseph went to the temple in Jerusalem to offer a sacrifice and present their newborn son, Jesus. The sacrifice would cleanse Mary from the impurities of labor and delivery and pay for her sin. But, the ritual was only a sign. While performing the temple sacrifice, Mary's faith in the Savior she held in her arms would cleanse her. The couple brought a pair of young birds for the offering—the price required for the poor. Though Mary and Joseph gave the priest a meager sacrifice according to what they could afford, God had provided them the true offering who was of utmost value.

Mary and Joseph readied Jesus to present Him before the Lord. God commanded this act in Exodus 13:2 when He called for the consecration of every firstborn male. "To consecrate" means "to set apart, anoint, or bless." Mary and Joseph were to dedicate Jesus to God as all firstborn sons were. The presentation of the firstborn in the temple was a ritual that reenacted Passover, when the Israelites, God's chosen people, were saved from slavery in Egypt. During Passover, the Israelites painted blood from a spotless, male lamb on their doorposts. By this sign, the firstborn sons of Israel were protected from the judgment of God. But, the sons of Egyptians, who remained hardened and disobedient, perished. Because of God's mercy, the Israelites were able to escape Pharaoh's oppressive rule and journey toward the land God promised them. To remember the Passover, Jewish firstborn sons were brought into the temple, presented, and redeemed by the sacrifice of the firstborn from their livestock. Baby Jesus would be presented just like other members in His community and covered from the wrath of God. But, ultimately,

Jesus would not be spared. About thirty-three years from His presentation in the temple, Jesus would die and pay the penalty for sin as the true spotless Lamb so that God's people would be saved from judgment.

When Mary and Joseph entered the temple, Simeon, a devout man of God, was there and, under revelation from the Holy Spirit, knew this dedication was not a regular one. Instead, Simeon believed this ritual was the consecration of the true firstborn Son of God. He took Jesus into his arms because He was the precious Savior. He had waited years to see the Lord's salvation and now witnessed this amazing sight. Simeon quoted Old Testament passages to show the Lord had been faithful to His word. For instance, he referred to Isaiah 42:6, which states, "I am the Lord. I have called you for a righteous purpose, and I will hold you by your hand. I will watch over you, and I will appoint you to be a covenant for the people and a light to the nations." This verse, written by the prophet Isaiah, speaks of the Anointed One, the Messiah, who would fulfill God's promises. In other words, the covenant promise of blessing in the presence of God would be accomplished through the Savior. Furthermore, the Lord Himself declared that He would set apart the Messiah to bring salvation and light, not only for the Jewish people but for all nations. This truth would redeem the lost sons and daughters from Jerusalem to the ends of the earth (Isaiah 49:6).

Joining Simeon in his joy, Anna, a prophetess who served and worshiped in the temple, also praised God for Jesus. Like Simeon, Anna was an old servant of the Lord who had longed for the coming Savior. Through her weary sight, she gazed upon Jesus and was moved to proclaim His presence to others. In a culture where the word of women was considered unreliable and widows were ignored, God used an elderly widow to preach the good news and the arrival of His kingdom. Throughout redemptive history, God used the unlikely, the weak, and the vulnerable for His great purposes.

Though Mary and Joseph came to the temple with a lowly animal offering, they also came with Jesus. Like them, there is nothing we can offer God that will be enough to pay for our sin. Our righteousness will never be sufficient, and our good works will be as filthy rags in God's sight. But, through our faith in Jesus, God credits the perfect works of His firstborn Son to us. God provided the offering for His people. Jesus's death on the cross was the true sacrifice and payment for sin. His righteous blood has covered us from the punishment we deserved and brought into freedom. Mary and Joseph carried Jesus into the presence of God in the temple, but Jesus carries us into a relationship with the Father. When He comes again, Jesus will bring ultimate joy to our souls. Like Simeon and Anna, we need to be watchful and long for Him until then.

> " **GOD PROVIDED THE OFFERING FOR HIS PEOPLE.**

day two questions

Simeon said Jesus was destined to be "a sign that will be opposed" (Luke 2:34). What do you think this phrase means? How does this opposition play a role in Jesus's redemptive mission?

Scripture describes Jesus as Israel's consolation or comfort. How does Jesus comfort you?

Anna did not let her status or age stop her from proclaiming the good news about Jesus. Have you ever let these things discourage you from spreading the gospel? How can the story of Anna inspire you?

DAY 3

> "
> HE DRAWS NEAR TO US IN OUR BROKENNESS AND COVERS OUR SHAME WITH HIS PERFECTION.

Jesus Growing Up

READ LUKE 2:51-52

When we think of the life of Christ, we often fast-forward to His teaching ministry. We think about a dove descending from heaven, sermons to His followers, or His life, death, and resurrection. But we do not often think about Jesus's youth or early teen years. This may be because we do not have many stories from His childhood. We do not know the answers to questions like: What did He do for fun? Who were His friends? What was His favorite animal, color, or food? Although we do not have these details from His childhood, we do have everything we need to know for life spent in godliness according to His Word.

When Jesus was young, His dad took the family and fled to Egypt, on the run from the evil King Herod. Jesus was an exile, fleeing from a powerful ruler who wanted Him dead. He lived with people who ate differently, spoke differently, and lived differently than His parents. Did Jesus know as a toddler that people were trying to kill Him? Or that thousands of little boys were killed as king Herod searched for Him?

Can you imagine what it was like having Jesus as an older brother? To have a brother who never responded harshly, even when provoked? A brother who never had selfish tantrums and only spoke kindly to His sisters? Who never lied or disobeyed His parents? Who was perfectly meek toward His siblings while somehow perfectly just? Jesus, the flawless brother, was perfectly peaceful, completely loving, and wise beyond His years. Most children already struggle with inferiority complexes toward their older siblings, but Jesus's brothers and sisters literally had the perfect brother. Did they wonder at His perfection, or did it make them mad that He was better than them? Did they look up to Him or pick on Him?

Or can you imagine having a perfect son? A son who was never selfish or proud, even when His mom recounted His birth story to Him—a story filled with wonders and angels and gifts of gold. A son who cared for the Father's glory and the good of those around Him. A son who never over-indulged in food or games. Who never lashed out in frustration when tired or melted down in anger when hungry. Perfect, and mysteriously, still learning and growing. The human mind, and especially today's exasperated mom, cannot possibly comprehend such a child.

Even while growing up, when hungry or hurt or while going through puberty, Jesus never sinned. Think for a moment about all of the commands moms give their children: Eat your food. Change your clothes. Share your toys. Be back by dinnertime. Usually, these motherly commands are met with resistance, reluctance, or delay. "No" is one of the first words children learn, and they are quick to exercise their demands or desires. And which mom has never heard the infamous "Sure mom, in a minute" excuse, only to find out that a minute really means never?

Jesus, however, perfectly obeyed His parents. If His mom told him to wash His dirty feet before coming into the house, He did it without grumbling. If His dad told him to share His toy animal or to help feed the livestock, He did not complain. Instead, He joyfully submitted to His parents and was obedient to them. Never once did He bite one of His siblings or steal a toy. Never. He never yelled in sinful anger at His brothers or stole a sweet from the treat jar without permission. He never looked lustfully at a woman, even with teenage hormones. He never sinned and perfectly obeyed His parents as unto the Lord.

Understandably, His mother was perplexed by Jesus and "kept all these things in her heart" (Luke 2:48-52). Even after an angel had appeared to her years earlier, she was still coming to terms with the fact that she had a perfect Son, who was God incarnate. Her son, Jesus, was born miraculously while she was still a virgin. He never sinned and perfectly obeyed. But over a decade of normal living had been filled with the everyday moments of eating, playing, and growing. Although His parents were aware Jesus was different, they did not fully understand His role in salvific history or the implications of His life.

Our Savior lived a human childhood. He grew in wisdom and stature, and He experienced life on earth. He felt hunger, got boo-boos, and played with mean kids. He embraced the whole of human experience and perfectly submitted to the authority figures in His life. Jesus knew the Father and had a unique relationship with Him that His parents did not fully comprehend. He was one with the Father, even as a young boy.

At the beginning of His life and ministry, the people of Israel responded favorably to Jesus. Sometimes we too can view Jesus favorably when life is going well or want some kind of blessing from Him. But when He does things that perplex us or when we do not understand what He is doing, will we still follow Him? Do we feel condemned by His holiness or drawn to it? Is our worship of God based on our own approval of His actions or out of trust in His goodness?

Jesus is now living in heaven, interceding for His children. He is perfect, holy, and worthy of worship. He draws near to us in our brokenness and covers our shame with His perfection. His ways are perfect, and He is always working out the Father's will in our lives. He is trustworthy, and He is good.

day three questions

Read Hebrews 5:8-9. How does this show the obedience of Jesus as He grew physically?

Think through some of the specific sins of your childhood. Be specific.
Now worship God in awe over the fact that He never sinned.

Write a prayer of worship to Jesus for His perfect life.

DAY 4

> WE MARVEL AT OUR YOUNG SAVIOR, WHO NOW SITS IN THE FATHER'S HOUSE BUT WILL MAKE WAY FOR MAN TO DWELL WITH THE FATHER FOREVER.

Discussing Scripture with Scholars

READ LUKE 2:39-50

As Jesus grew, He grew as any child would, both physically and intellectually. What made His childhood unique is the connection He had with the Lord. Luke is specific that the grace of God was upon Jesus as He grew. God's grace, or divine favor, was boasted by the angels in the shepherds' fields, and we see it present with Jesus as He ages. His connection with the Lord is seen more as Jesus and His family travel to Jerusalem.

Every year, both Mary and Joseph would take a three-day journey to Jerusalem to celebrate the Passover. The Passover was a required celebration for the Jews, and it involved a seven-day festival praising and honoring God for the liberation of the Jews from Egypt. For both Mary and Joseph to do this every year shows their dedication to this celebration. Luke is also specific that Jesus was twelve years old. When Jewish boys turned twelve, they were considered men by Jewish custom. They were designated as "sons of the Law," which meant they were to uphold the obligations of the Law and were to learn under the Law. It was common for parents to bring their sons to the Passover festival, so Mary and Joseph took Jesus with them to Jerusalem.

When Jesus's family finished the festival, they started their journey back to Nazareth. Unaware that Jesus was not with them, they did not realize until a day had gone by that Jesus was missing. Returning to Jerusalem, they searched for Him for three days before finding Him in the temple.

Luke records that Jesus was sitting among the teachers in the temple. This detail shows us the humility of Jesus. He was not usurping the authority of the teachers by seeking to instruct them, but He participated in their conversation by asking questions and providing answers. The teachers were shocked by Jesus's understanding of the Law and the answers He gave to their questions. To have such depth of knowledge of the Law by the age of twelve meant that Jesus was very familiar with the teachings of the Law. His increasing wisdom is on full display as He speaks with the teachers.

While the teachers are astonished at Jesus's knowledge, Mary and Joseph are astonished that Jesus was in the temple. Jesus's location may seem puzzling to His parents but not Jesus. Jesus responds to Mary's question of concern by saying that He needed to be in His Father's house. Here we see a contrast between two things: His earthly house and the house of God and His earthly father and His heavenly Father. Jesus is not disrespectful to His parents by choosing the temple and His heavenly Father as His priority. Rather, He is demonstrating His dedication to the Lord. The end of the text reveals that his parents did not understand what He was saying to them, but as time would progress and Jesus's earthly mission would begin, their understanding would grow.

Luke 2:49 reads, "my Father's house," but can also be translated, "be involved in my Father's interests." As the Son of God, Jesus recognized that His life's purpose was to realize His heavenly Father's interests. His understanding of this as a twelve-year-old shows that He understood His life's purpose at a young age. Jesus's first spoken words in the gospel of Luke identify His unique relationship with God. By His words, He claimed that it was not Joseph who was His true Father but God. Throughout His earthly ministry, He would continue to speak on His intimate connection with the Lord, identifying Him as His Father. To claim that God was His Father communicated equality with God. Jesus was not just the Son of God; He was also God. He fully shares in the deity and glory the Father possesses.

Jesus's dedication to His Father's interests speaks to His obedience to do His Father's will. He was utterly focused on fulfilling His purpose. Jesus was fully invested in God's plan of redemption to save His people. His intimate relationship with His Father was not just for Himself but would be shared with others. Those who would put their faith in Him would be brought into the family of God, calling God their heavenly Father as well.

As we read this text, we receive a glimpse of what Christ's ministry on Earth will look like. His dedication to the Father would be evident throughout His life and brought to culmination by His death on a cross. But as we move toward that event, we pause now to consider the obedience of a boy who would change everything. We marvel at our young Savior, who now sits in the Father's house but will make way for man to dwell with the Father forever.

> **JESUS WAS NOT JUST THE SON OF GOD; HE WAS ALSO GOD.**

day four questions

Why did Mary and Joseph not understand Jesus's words to them?

How would Jesus's understanding of the Law prepare Him to engage with others about it during His ministry?

Why is it important that Jesus spoke about His relationship with the Father? How would this set Him apart from other people?

Reflection

REVIEW ALL PASSAGES FROM THE LAST 4 DAYS

Summarize the main points from this week's Scripture readings.

What did you observe from this week's passages about the life of Jesus and His character?

What do this week's passages reveal about the condition of mankind and yourself?

How do these passages point to the gospel?

How should you respond to these Scriptures? What specific action steps can you take this week to apply them in your life?

Write a prayer in response to your study of God's Word. Adore God for who He is, confess sins He revealed in your own life, ask Him to empower you to walk in obedience, and pray for anyone who comes to mind as you study.

DAY 5

> OUR DELIGHT IN CHRIST'S GRACIOUSNESS AND BELIEF IN HIM AS OUR SAVIOR WILL LEAD US TO DEEPER LOVE FOR HIM.

Jesus's Family and Birthplace

READ LUKE 2:39-40, LUKE 4:16-30, MATTHEW 13:53-58

After Jesus teaches a series of parables about the kingdom of God, He takes a journey with His disciples back to His hometown of Nazareth. While many biblical towns are mentioned frequently in Scripture because of their significance, Nazareth is not. In fact, the Old Testament never mentions it. One of the only descriptions we have is found when Nathanael, one of Jesus's disciples, first learns where Jesus is from. Nathanael snidely remarks, "Can anything good come out of Nazareth?" (John 1:46). Obviously, this is not a town many Israelites hold in high esteem, and yet it is the one that our Savior chose to make His home. The Old Testament prophets foretold that the Messiah would be despised, and Jesus came from a despised place of birth, fulfilling what they said (Isaiah 53:3).

When Jesus arrived in Nazareth, He went to the synagogue on the Sabbath to teach. During the Sabbath, the people would go to the synagogue to pray, worship, and hear passages read from the Law and the Prophets by various teachers. When Jesus begins to teach, He reads a messianic prophecy from the scroll of Isaiah to reveal who He is. Jesus is the Anointed One of God. He will "preach good news to the poor," "proclaim release to the captives," "[bring] recovery of sight to the blind," "set free the oppressed," and "proclaim the year of the Lord's favor" (Isaiah 61:1-2, Luke 4:18). Jesus has come to free sinners from the bondage they cannot escape on their own. He will open their eyes to the truth and give them freedom and rest in Himself. When Jesus says that He has come to "proclaim the year of the Lord's favor," He is referring to the year of Jubilee. Jubilee was something that the Israelites were commanded to observe every fifty years. All debts would be canceled and all slaves set free. There would even be a rest from working the land. Jesus is the fulfillment of Jubilee. He canceled our debt and set us free from slavery to sin by bearing our sins on the cross. He has given us rest in the present age, and He will guide us into eternal rest in heaven.

After Jesus reads the prophecy to the people, He tells them that it has been fulfilled that very day. He was the promised Messiah who had come to deliver them. The people were astonished (Matthew 13:54). Many who sat before Jesus had probably watched Him grow up or had even grown up with Him. Now, Joseph and Mary witnessed their son teach with authority and display miraculous powers (Matthew 13:54, Mark 6:2). You can almost imagine the people of Nazareth looking around the room at each other in shock and wonder.

Jesus sat down after reading the prophecy and continued to teach them about what it said, and the people sat in awe as He spoke. Luke tells us that His words were "gracious" (Luke 4:22). Jesus spoke of God's loving-kindness toward them. The Lord was fulfilling His promise of a Messiah. And yet, as they listened to Jesus and were amazed, they remembered how familiar He was to them: "Isn't this Joseph's son?" (Luke 4:22). They must have glanced toward Jesus's mother and brothers and sisters, who were present in the room that day as well (Matthew 13:55). The Messiah prophesied in Isaiah was supposed to be a king from the line of David, but Jesus was the son of an ordinary carpenter from their town. He had always just been one of them—how could He be anything else? The people of Nazareth began to take offense to Jesus. They focused on His humanity and familiarity, and they forgot what had previously astonished them. Scripture tells us that even Jesus's brothers did not believe that He was the Messiah (John 7:5).

Jesus revealed Himself to the people who He had shared most of His life with, even His own family, and yet they refused to believe Him because He was so familiar to them. Their pride and unbelief kept them from experiencing miracles by His hand and the fulfillment of joy from Isaiah's prophecy. As we seek to know Jesus more, let us remember who He is and not let Him become someone we are "used to." Our delight in Christ's graciousness and belief in Him as our Savior will lead us to deeper love for Him, and we will see Him move and work in mighty ways.

> " **JESUS HAS COME TO FREE SINNERS FROM THE BONDAGE THEY CANNOT ESCAPE ON THEIR OWN.**

day five questions

How have we been like the people of Nazareth and Jesus's family in being too "used to" Jesus? How has Jesus shown us His loving-kindness despite this?

Read Mark 3:21. What else did Jesus's brothers think of Him? How might it have been hard to have grown up with Jesus as a sibling?

Read Acts 1:14. What is different in this verse from the passage you read today? How does this give us hope for the people in our lives who respond to Jesus in unbelief?

DAY 6

> "
> WE ARE LOVED
> AND ACCEPTED
> BY THE FATHER
> THROUGH CHRIST.

Jesus's Baptism

READ JOHN 1:29-34

John the Baptist was an interesting man. He was unkempt and dirty, smelling of sweat and eating locusts and honey in the wilderness. He wore scratchy, simple clothes made of camel's hair and spent a lot of time alone in the wilderness. Yet even with all his idiosyncrasies, this wild man attracted quite a following. For hundreds of years, God seemed silent. Now, He had spoken through the prophet John, and people were curious.

The Israelites began leaving their towns to travel out into the wilderness to listen to what John had to say. At this time, a trip to the countryside was not a nice escape or vacation. There were no modern conveniences or accessible rest stops. People would pack up their food and belongings and venture out into the desert, seemingly hungrier for a word from the Lord than for a comforting meal in their homes.

One day, while the crowd was gathered and John was baptizing people in the Jordan river, he saw Jesus coming and proclaimed, "Look, the Lamb of God, who takes away the sin of the world!" If we have been Christians for a while, the phrase "Lamb of God" might be all too familiar for us. We may not fully understand it, but we recognize its importance and have grown accustomed to its presence. The title "Lamb of God" is more than a mysterious, throw-away phrase, however. The Bible is full of imagery using animal sacrifices, and this title is rich with biblical history.

Think back to the beginning of the Bible with the first animal sacrifice in the garden of Eden, when God killed an animal to provide a covering for Adam and Eve. The sin of Adam and Eve revealed their nakedness and guilt. They had hidden in shame, but God covered them through the blood of an animal. Or consider the trembling hands of Abraham as he was moments away from sacrificing his son on the altar, only to notice a ram stuck in the nearby bristles. At the right moment, God provided an animal sacrifice for his servant that saved Isaac.

We can also point to the Passover, as God's people were set free from slavery. God told His people to kill a lamb and put its blood over their doorposts, protecting them from the angel of death who would pass over by night. Those who did not have this blood over their doorposts would lose their oldest child, but the lamb's blood saved the people from death.

Finally, we remember the sacrificial system and the Day of Atonement in Leviticus 16. According to Levitical law, two goats were gathered for this festival. The Israelites offered one as a sacrifice to the Lord; its blood sprinkled on behalf of the people's sins. The other was known as the scapegoat, bearing the people's sins and cast out into the desert. What rich imagery of animal sacrifice we have throughout the Bible!

Within this context, Jesus, at the Jordan River, is called the Lamb of God. John is able to identify Jesus as the Lamb of God because he saw the Holy Spirit come down like a dove from heaven and rest on Him. John explained that God had told him that is how he would identify the Son of God. John's proclamation also fulfills Messianic prophecy from Isaiah 11:2 that says "The Spirit of the Lord will rest on him." John could say with certainty that Jesus was the long awaited Lamb of God, who takes away the sins of the world.

Jesus is the Lamb of God, and on the cross, He became the Passover Lamb, the spotless sacrifice. He became the "docile lamb led to slaughter" (Jeremiah 11:19). He was oppressed and afflicted, led like a lamb to its death (Isaiah 53:7-10). He was struck for the rebellion of the people, and the Lord crushed Him as a guilt offering, accomplishing His purposes of redemption for the world. He was the once for all sacrifice, coming in a non-assuming, not-presumptuous manner. The Lamb's blood was poured out in costly love, offering freedom to all who believe in Him.

Today, we can rejoice because the Lamb of God has come! He has made a way for us to be right with the Father. Jesus's perfect sacrifice covers all who repent and believe in Him, and God holds our sins against us no more. As we confess our sins to the Lord and repent in faith, God covers us with Jesus's perfection. We no longer need to fear or live lives of relentless striving. We are loved and accepted by the Father through Christ.

Just as John's entire life pointed to the coming Messiah, so our lives should also point as a signpost to our Savior. This Lamb, the sacrifice for our sins, is the God Almighty, and He is coming again. He is the triumphant Lamb of Revelation 7:17, 17:14. He is the Lamb who makes us clean and who will proclaim victory as King of kings and Lord of lords. He is the Savior, our Passover Lamb. He is worthy of all glory and honor and power. Worthy is the Lamb!

> **JESUS TRULY WAS THE LAMB OF GOD, WHO TAKES AWAY THE SINS OF THE WORLD.**

day six questions

Read Isaiah 53:7-10. How do these verses expand your understanding of the phrase "Lamb of God?"

Our salvation was costly, and repentance is painfully specific. Identify specific areas of sin in your life, from doubt to rebellion, and confess them to the Lord today, receiving His grace.

The Lamb of God has come to take away the world's sin, yet we often try to erase our guilt on our own. What are other ways that you try to cover your sins? Examples include over-working, perfectionism, and denial.

DAY 7

THE CHRISTIAN LIFE
IS NOT WITHOUT
SPIRITUAL CONFLICT.

The Temptation of Jesus

READ MATTHEW 4:1-11

The narrative loses no time in jumping to the next event in Jesus's life following His baptism. The Spirit of God who descended upon Christ immediately calls Jesus into the Judean wilderness where He will fast for forty days, and Satan will tempt Him.

This serves as a reminder to us that spiritual warfare is very active and real. And while it is not wise to obsess over the presence of Satan and demonic beings, it is also not wise to ignore their influence. There is a reason why when we experience spiritual growth, there is often an immediate "bump in the road" or failure. Satan does not want us to know and live in the abundance of joy, love, and peace from our unbreakable union with Christ. And because we are united with Christ, we should expect some of the same trials that He faced (John 15:18). The Christian life is not without spiritual conflict.

Satan begins to tempt Christ by asking Him to prove that He is the Son of God by turning some of the desert stones into bread. Instead of giving in to hunger and using His power as the Son of God for selfish purposes, Jesus refuses Satan and rebukes Him with the Word of God, a weapon that is available to every single man or woman who chooses to follow Christ. Jesus tells Satan that instead of depending on food, man should live "by every word that comes from the mouth of God" (Matthew 4:4, Deuteronomy 8:3). Jesus could have created food out of thin air, but He accepted His circumstance of hunger from the Lord's hand and trusted that His Father would provide for Him.

Jesus has just defeated one temptation with God's Word, and Satan will use Scripture in his next temptation. It is frightening to think that Satan knows the Bible better than most believers, but he treats it with contempt and misuses it for evil. Satan tells Jesus to prove He is the Son of God by throwing Himself off the highest pinnacle of the temple. Satan quotes from Psalm 91:11-12 and says that if Jesus does this, surely the angels of God will keep His foot from even hitting the ground. This would then show everyone He was really the Son of God. However, Satan uses this text incorrectly and even omits words to twist its true meaning, but He responds with Scripture again and tells Satan that He will not put God to the test. Jesus uses the Word of God correctly, and He discerns Satan's wicked intent.

Finally, Satan tells Jesus that he will give Him all the world's kingdoms if He will only bow down and worship him. Satan offered Jesus access to earthly glory without having to endure the cross. Jesus rebukes him again and tells him to leave because worship belongs to the Lord alone. Jesus's kingdom will not be of this world, and He will endure the cross with joy for the sake of His people (Hebrews 12:2). Satan leaves, and angels come and minister to Jesus. Jesus did not need to jump off the temple for them to appear! They were there all along.

When Satan first approached Jesus to tempt Him, he used a familiar tactic. He questioned the words of God, particularly the ones spoken at Christ's baptism, and beckoned Jesus to prove His deity and Sonship. As we read Satan's taunting, we hear echoes of the familiar question the crafty serpent asked Adam and Eve so long ago: "Did God really say..." (Genesis 3:1). The serpent is repeating what he did to the first humans God created. He is trying to thwart God's redemptive plan, but Jesus is the greater Adam, and even though Satan tempts Him, He will not give into sin. Jesus does what the first Adam could not do and answers every one of Satan's temptations in dependence on the Spirit of God and with the very words of God. His righteousness brings life instead of death, caused by the first Adam's rebellion (Romans 5:12-21). Jesus obeys His Father and overcomes the schemes of the enemy.

The temptation of Christ reminds us that our Savior identifies with us in our struggle against sin. He has felt what we have felt, and He understands our burden. He wants us to cry out to Him as we face temptation, knowing that He gives us His strength and righteousness to defeat the enemy (Hebrews 4:14-16). This also shows us that being faced with temptation is not sinful but the inevitable result of living in a fallen world. It is how we respond to the temptation that determines whether our actions are sinful or not. Praise God that Jesus was and is our righteous substitute. He has done what none of us could ever do and has defeated the power of sin. As we wrestle with sin while trying to pattern our lives after His, let us have joy in knowing Jesus will one day free us from the presence of sin forever. At that time, we will enter into His eternal kingdom, which will be far better than any earthly kingdom of this world.

> **THE TEMPTATION OF CHRIST REMINDS US THAT OUR SAVIOR IDENTIFIES WITH US IN OUR STRUGGLE AGAINST SIN.**

day seven questions

Contrast the setting of Jesus's baptism in Matthew 3 to the setting of Jesus's temptation in Matthew 4:1-11. What differences do you notice, and why are these important?

How does seeing Jesus defeat Satan with Scripture encourage you in your pursuit of God's Word?

How should you live in light of knowing that Jesus who defeated Satan?

DAY 8

> ALL THAT IS NEEDED FOR US TO HAVE A RELATIONSHIP WITH GOD IS TO TURN FROM OUR SIN AND HAVE FAITH IN JESUS.

Jesus's Ministry and Message

READ MARK 1:14-15

At this point in Jesus's life, Jesus had been private about who He was, and His ministry was not publicly known. Christ's baptism marked the anointing of His ministry, and His temptation in the wilderness empowered Him for His ministry. Now the day has arrived for Him to officially begin.

The text is clear that it was after John was arrested that Jesus began His ministry. This detail may seem small, but it is significant. John the Baptist was chosen by God to prophetically proclaim the coming of Jesus and prepare the way for Him. John was obedient to this calling and fulfilled his mission by preparing the people's hearts to receive Jesus. He had announced the coming Christ, and now Jesus would make His presence known.

Jesus begins His ministry in Galilee by proclaiming the good news of God. This good news is the good news of great joy the angels sang about in the shepherd fields. The good news of the gospel was here, and it was Jesus Himself. God spoke about the good news of a future deliverer through the prophets in the Old Testament, and now the time is here for those prophecies to be fulfilled. Paul speaks of this reality in Galatians 4:4-5 when he says, "When the time came to completion, God sent his Son, born of a woman, born under the law, to redeem those under the law, so that we might receive adoption as sons." The long period of waiting is now over. Jesus Christ is here. The uniqueness of God's timing is displayed in these verses. The story of redemption has been building throughout the pages of Scripture. Every page speaks to the eager awaiting of God's timing. God demonstrates His faithfulness to His people by fulfilling what He has promised. His timing is perfect. Jesus publicly proclaims that the time has been fulfilled. This would have caused the heads of the Jews to turn and their ears to perk up. They had read of the promised Messiah as they studied the Law and prophets. Could it really be that the words they have read have been fulfilled?

Jesus also proclaims that the kingdom of God has come near. John the Baptist also declared this message in his ministry by telling people that the kingdom of God was at hand. But what does this mean? The kingdom of God in the Old Testament referred to God's rule and reign. As King, He was the ruler of all creation whose kingdom consisted of the entire world. But His kingdom had another component. The phrase "kingdom of God" also refers to a messianic kingdom, an eternal kingdom. The kings throughout the Old Testament point to a King who would take up His rule and reign. He would not only save the people from their sins but bring people into His eternal kingdom by their faith in Him. Declaring that the kingdom of God was near was to say the way to enter into God's kingdom was coming. Mark uses a specific verb for "near" to describe a spatial reality, meaning someone was bringing the kingdom close physically. It was the presence of Jesus that made the kingdom near.

What is the response to this good news? Repent and believe. Through these two words, Jesus outlines the necessary elements that play a part in the believer's conversion. The first step is repentance. Repentance is not just grief over one's sin. It is an acknowledgment that their sin separates them from God and that they must turn away from it to walk with Christ. The second is belief. There must be a belief in who Jesus is and what He does for those who trust in Him. It is only because of Jesus that forgiveness of sins is possible. Those who trust in Him and turn away from their sins are brought into the kingdom of God. These words of Jesus show the essence of the message of the ministry. Jesus was all about the gospel. He will not spend the duration of His ministry concerned about earthly matters and messages. All that He would say and do would be about the good news of the gospel.

Jesus's message of salvation is clear: repent and believe. There is no addition to this gospel message. Many people in our day and age try to twist the words of Jesus to speak a false gospel. But Jesus's message of salvation is specific. It is not "repent and believe plus follow all of these rules," or "repent and believe but never mess up, or you are out." The message of the gospel is simple—so simple that it almost seems too easy. But that is what makes the gospel good news. All that is needed for us to have a relationship with God is to turn from our sin and have faith in Jesus.

How good it is that we have a King who desires to share His kingdom with His people! As believers, we serve a faithful God who has kept His promise to make a way to bring His people to Himself. Just like Jesus, let us be people who are all about the gospel. Let us not be concerned with the temporal matters of this world but fix our eyes on the eternal kingdom. Let us declare the good news of our great King.

> **WHAT IS THE RESPONSE TO THIS GOOD NEWS? REPENT AND BELIEVE.**

day eight questions

How does this passage speak to you about the faithfulness of the Lord?
How does this encourage you to trust His timing?

What does it say about the character of God that He desires to bring us into His kingdom?

How have you seen the message of the gospel twisted to be more than what Christ has said?
Why is it important to understand the gospel exactly as Christ presented it?

DAY 9

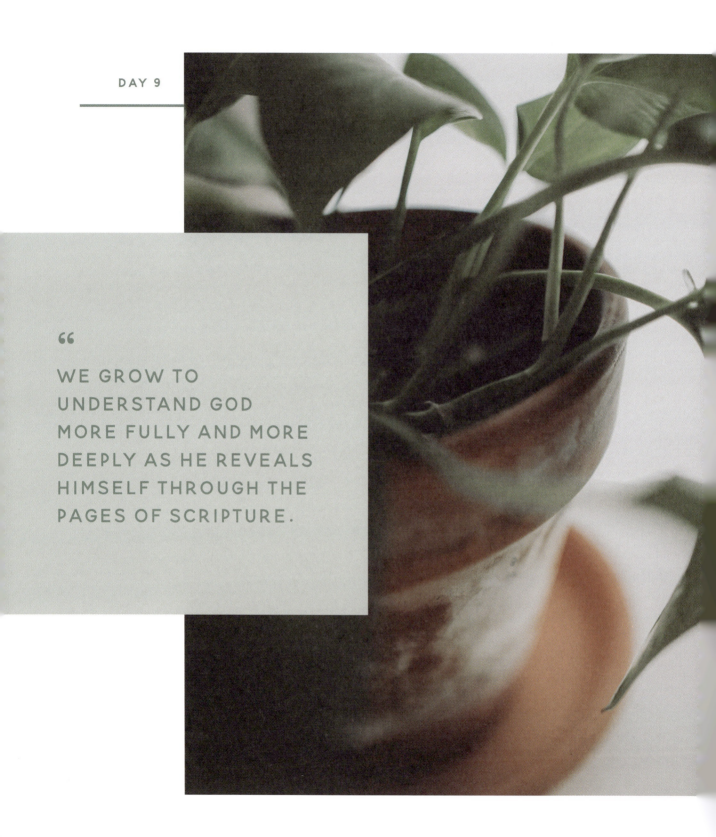

" WE GROW TO UNDERSTAND GOD MORE FULLY AND MORE DEEPLY AS HE REVEALS HIMSELF THROUGH THE PAGES OF SCRIPTURE.

Jesus the Eternal Word

READ JOHN 1

The gospel of John begins differently than the other gospels. There is no mention of the genealogy of Jesus nor His birth. Instead, John recognizes the entrance of Jesus in eternity past—in the very beginning before all came to be. This answers the question of Jesus's existence before His infancy. John points us to the very beginning where Jesus is in a harmonious relationship with God. Understanding Jesus's involvement from the start of time brings us to a greater understanding of His divinity. Not only was He with God, but He is also God. He participated in creating the universe, and it was through Him by which all was made. Not one thing was created apart from Him.

Jesus is differentiated from God the Father and God the Spirit. Jesus is God the Son incarnate. Jesus is one with the Father and the Spirit in glory and substance, yet He is unique in that He has two natures—a human nature and a divine nature. The Son of God became flesh. He came to live and walk among us in human form, learning, growing, and facing life as anyone would. John refers to Jesus as the Eternal Word, highlighting Jesus's role as one who comes in the flesh to reveal God to the world. He not only lived His life and ministry speaking the words of God, but Jesus embodied all that the Scriptures say of who God is.

Can you imagine an interaction with the Eternal Word of God, Jesus? He perfectly recited and remembered Scripture. He corrected, rebuked, encouraged, and taught only with the words breathed out by Himself. The words He spoke gave flesh and bones to the Scriptures. His existence is a fulfillment of the prophesied words of the Old Testament. Clothed in humanity, the manifestation of a promise, coming near to God's people to reveal all He desired for mankind to know and understand. In fact, Hebrews points to Jesus's last words encompassing who He is as, "The Son is the radiance of God's glory and the exact expression of his nature, sustaining all things by his powerful word" (Hebrews 1:3). This proclamation serves as a seal to His life—that Jesus came to radiate the glory and truth of God everywhere He went, to everyone He encountered. He did not come as a sheer vessel for God to reveal His Word but as God and as the Eternal Word.

Jesus Christ, as the Eternal Word, gives a new perspective as we approach God's Word. Everything included in the Scriptures encompasses what Jesus Christ came to do. They are no longer distant words but words made flesh. Every promise, purpose, and plan is brought forth in Him. He brings every truth to life through living them—through enacting every instruction, obeying every command, loving perfectly, teaching truthfully, and walking faithfully. Because of Him, we now look to the pages of the Bible with profound hope. The salvation He brings enacts a transaction where we are saved from ourselves and saved to His righteousness. And that righteousness is not generic. It is a righteousness claimed by Christ through His perfect exemplification of God's Word. We not only learn about Jesus as we read, but we learn what was required of Him to credit His righteousness to us and how He equips us in every way to follow Him.

Jesus not only makes God accessible to us in written form but through His very life. We grow to understand God more fully and more deeply as He reveals Himself through the pages of Scripture and in our lives, which is only made possible through receiving salvation in Jesus Christ. It is only through Christ that God is fully known. Though nature and words reveal Him in ways, Jesus perfectly displays Him to the world. As John 14:6-7 confirms the excellent access we find in Christ, "I am the way, and the truth, and the life. No one comes to the Father except through me. If you know me, you also know my Father. From now on you know Him and have seen Him."

> " BECAUSE OF HIM, WE NOW LOOK TO THE PAGES OF THE BIBLE WITH PROFOUND HOPE.

day nine questions

What do we learn about Jesus's existence before His infant birth?

What hope do you find in the access to know God more fully and deeply through Jesus Christ?

How does this encourage you to study God's Word more faithfully?

DAY 10

> THE SPIRIT'S GIFT OF FAITH IS NECESSARY TO TESTIFY OF GOD'S GOODNESS.

Testimony of John

READ JOHN 1:19-34

John the Baptist was the cousin of Jesus. Before John's birth, an angel of the Lord declared to his father that John would have "the spirit and power of Elijah" (Luke 1:17). Elijah was a great prophet in the Old Testament. He called out pagan worship among the Israelites, encouraged people to serve the one true God, and confronted the corrupt rulers of his time. Like Elijah, John would be used by God to call His people to repentance and prepare them for the Lord's coming. When John grew older, the Holy Spirit led him out to the Jordan River, and there, he baptized people in the water. He accompanied his baptism ministry with a message to turn from sin and toward God. John was causing a movement, as his preaching convicted many people. The Pharisees, who were the Jewish authority and religious scholars in Jerusalem, were suspicious of John's ministry. They sent priests to the Jordan River to investigate.

According to the Pharisees, John was a renegade preacher who may need to be stopped. They confronted John and asked him for his identity, trying to see if John was claiming divine authority for his work. But, the biblical author who recorded this account emphasized John's humility. Scripture states, "He didn't deny it but confessed: 'I am not the Messiah'" (John 1:20). The Israelites believed the Messiah was to be the promised Savior who would deliver God's people. First predicted in Genesis 3:15, the Messiah was the Anointed Son, sent from heaven, would defeat evil, forgive sin, bring God's kingdom, and fulfill the covenant promises. But John the Baptist was not this man. The priests went on to ask if he was the prophet Elijah back in the flesh. They had in mind verses like Malachi 4:5, which states, "Look, I am going to send you Elijah the prophet before the great and terrible day of the Lord comes." Rather than understanding its spiritual truth, they had misinterpreted this prophecy as a prediction of Elijah's physical return. John the Baptist was not Elijah. But, he was someone like

Elijah who came right before the greater arrival of the Lord. Finally, the priests asked if John was "the Prophet" (John 1:21). According to Deuteronomy 18:15, the Jewish people looked for a prophet like Moses, who delivered the Israelites out of slavery in Egypt and met face to face with God. But, John knew Moses foreshadowed the true Deliverer who would save God's people from slavery and sin, and so he denied their question.

Like lawyers in a courtroom trial, the priests pressed John further to reveal his identity, and he testified to the truth. He proclaimed the words of the Old Testament prophet Isaiah. He referred to Isaiah 40:3, which says, "A voice of one crying out: 'Prepare the way of the Lord in the wilderness; make a straight highway for our God in the desert.'" John said he was the voice calling to make a path for the Lord's coming. And, he applied this passage, which awaits the arrival of the eternal God, to the arrival of Jesus among them. God had come in the flesh, and John's baptism ministry by water made a people ready for Jesus's baptism by the Spirit. People saw water baptism as ritual cleansing that exposed the need to be cleansed inwardly from the pollution of sin. John the Baptist continued this sign by preaching a message of faith in Jesus. John testified that Jesus was Messiah and the only one who could truly purify and restore God's people.

The next day, John's testimony culminated with telling the crowd about the revelation he received from the Lord. God had told John to baptize with water so that the Messiah would be revealed. John knew Jesus as his cousin, but on his own, John did not have an understanding of who Jesus really was. John testified of the miraculous work of the Spirit to open his eyes. John spoke of witnessing the Holy Spirit anoint Jesus and identify Him as the Son of God (John 1:33).

Because of divine revelation, John's testimony was true. He was dependent on the Spirit of God to empower him in his baptism ministry and show him that Jesus was the Messiah. Likewise, we, too, are dependent on the Holy Spirit to reveal to us the truth of Jesus Christ. Dead in sin, we cannot know this truth in our own ability. Instead, the Spirit of God must make us alive so we can understand and receive the saving work of Jesus Christ. The Spirit's gift of faith is necessary to testify of God's goodness. Through faith in Jesus, we are new creations and are empowered to live in His ways. Let us proclaim Jesus's accomplishment on the cross during His first coming and always have our hearts ready for His second.

> " WE, TOO, ARE DEPENDENT ON THE HOLY SPIRIT TO REVEAL TO US THE TRUTH OF JESUS CHRIST.

day ten questions

Read Matthew 3:7-10. To what truth does John the Baptist testify in these verses?

John again echoed the words of Isaiah when he said, "Here is the Lamb of God, who takes away the sin of the world" (John 1:29). Look up and read Isaiah 53. What does Isaiah 53 reveal about how Jesus, the Lamb of God, would remove sin from God's people?

In what ways can you "prepare a way" in your heart for Jesus's second coming?

Reflection

REVIEW ALL PASSAGES FROM THE LAST 6 DAYS

Summarize the main points from this week's Scripture readings.

What did you observe from this week's passages about the life of Jesus and His character?

What do this week's passages reveal about the condition of mankind and yourself?

How do these passages point to the gospel?

How should you respond to these Scriptures? What specific action steps can you take this week to apply them in your life?

Write a prayer in response to your study of God's Word. Adore God for who He is, confess sins He revealed in your own life, ask Him to empower you to walk in obedience, and pray for anyone who comes to mind as you study.

DAY 11

> IN THE DARKNESS OF SIN, THERE IS A VOICE THAT SAYS, "FOLLOW ME."

The First Disciples

READ LUKE 5:1-11

Jesus's teachings brought many people to gather and listen to Him. They were eager to hear more from this man, learn from His words, and ponder their message. Just like John had followers of his teachings, so would Jesus. In fact, John 1:37 tells us that some of John's disciples began following Jesus. But the disciples of Jesus were not just simple men. God chose them to carry out the message of the gospel during Jesus's ministry and after it as well. In this passage, we read who these disciples are and the mission they are called to fulfill.

On one particular day of teaching, the crowds gathering to listen to Jesus were so great that Jesus had to climb into a boat for everyone to see Him teach. This boat belonged to a fisherman named Simon Peter. As Jesus finishes His teaching, he asks Simon to direct the boat into deeper water and put out his nets to catch fish. The only thing is that Simon and his other men have already been doing this throughout the night, and they came up empty every time. So when Jesus asks this question, we cannot help but understand Simon's perplexity. He was the fisherman, the professional in this situation. Does Jesus not see that it is unlikely they will catch anything?

Nevertheless, Simon obliges. By calling Jesus "Master," he is acknowledging the authority of Jesus, but soon He would see much more. As soon as he let down the nets, they burst with fish, so many fish that the nets begin to break, and the boat begins to sink under the weight. This was not a coincidence — this was a miracle.

In response to this great act, Simon becomes aware of who is sitting in the boat with him. This man is not just a man; He is the Lord. The glory of Jesus shown in this miracle causes two reactions from Simon. The first is to fall on his knees before Jesus. To fall at someone's feet was an act of worship, a sign of submission to their authority. As Simon goes to his knees, He is recognizing and worshiping the glory of God. But the glory of

Jesus also causes Simon to acknowledge his sin. In comparison to Jesus, Simon falls short of His glory. Knowing this, Simon declares that Jesus must leave His presence because of his great sin.

But Jesus does not leave Simon Peter and the rest of the men. Instead, He tells him not to be afraid because his calling is being changed. No longer will he be a fisherman but a fisher of men. Simon Peter, James, and John are sinners, but Jesus chooses them to follow Him despite their sin. In this account, we receive a glimpse of a wondrous truth for all believers. We may feel like our sin is too great—that because of it, we are unworthy to be a follower of Christ. But there is no sin that is too great for God's grace to cover. Jesus also chose ordinary men with ordinary jobs to become His disciples. Their ordinary lives would not keep them from an extraordinary destiny. By becoming fishers of men, Jesus would involve them in His ministry in making disciples. This teaches us that no person is too sinful to be used by God. Simon felt unworthy to follow Jesus because of his sin, but Jesus chooses Him anyway. When God calls sinners to Him, nothing about them can stop His plan for them. No matter the sin or weakness.

What is the response of Simon and the rest of the men to Jesus? To leave everything behind and follow Jesus. They had spent years being fishermen, laboring hard to earn money for their boats and nets. But they would leave this all behind for Jesus. Their decision to abandon everything for Jesus reveals an important principle of following Christ that there is a cost to follow Him. For Simon and his friends, this was their job, but for each of us, this is different. We will all have to surrender something to follow Jesus, whether it be a group of friends who are leading us into sin or a sinful habit that we have clung to for so long. Complete abandonment for Christ is essential to follow Him because it reorients our hearts to pursue Him alone. While this is hard, the cost to follow Jesus is always worth it. Complete abandonment for Christ is a lifelong pursuit of the One who has poured His grace over us.

As we read of Christ's call to follow Him, the Bible reminds us of the same call Jesus makes to sinners. In the darkness of sin, there is a voice that says, "Follow me." All of us have this invitation from Christ. We can either see the greatness of our sin and choose to stay in it or see the outstretched hand of grace and decide to take it.

> " WE WILL ALL HAVE TO SURRENDER SOMETHING TO FOLLOW JESUS.

day eleven questions

What is the difference between viewing Jesus as master versus Lord? How should this impact our view of God?

What has following Jesus cost you? Is there a cost you have been avoiding that is keeping you from following Him?

How does it encourage you that God uses you despite your sin?

DAY 12

> "
> THIS WEDDING AT CANA IS ONLY A MERE GLIMPSE OF THE ULTIMATE WEDDING THAT IS TO COME, WHERE JESUS AND HIS CHURCH WILL BE UNITED FOREVER.

Jesus Turns Water to Wine

READ JOHN 2:1-11

Today's passage opens up with one of the most joyful celebrations: a wedding! At this point in history, wedding festivities would often last a week, and the groom was in charge of making sure the guests were taken care of properly. Culturally, failing to provide for the guests would be shameful for the groom. In the wedding festivities that Mary, Jesus, and His disciples are participating in, everything is going smoothly until one thing goes awry—the wine runs out.

Likely noticing how embarrassing this could be for the groom, Mary seems to try and do something about it. She turns to Jesus and tells Him of the situation. It is unclear what motivation Mary had in bringing this to the attention of Jesus. While knowing the power Jesus possesses, Mary most likely was not asking Him to do something miraculous. She had probably grown used to depending on Jesus, and with this issue springing up, believes He can do something to resolve it. However, Jesus's response is interesting in light of Mary's request. He simply asks why the matter concerns Him, and it is easy for us to read this response and think He is rude, especially with referring to Mary as "woman" at the end. This sentence is indeed meant to be a rebuke but a gentle rebuke. As we will soon see with His disciples, Jesus often has to guide people to truth by a rebuke. He does not mean to belittle Mary here; He is refocusing her on what matters.

This is why He adds something seemingly unrelated: "my time has not come yet." These words reveal that there is a deeper reality at play here. By referring to "my time," Jesus is speaking about His future death. Throughout His ministry, He will indicate the timing of His imminent death by either saying it has not come or that it has arrived. Being early in His ministry, it is not yet God's timing for His Son to die. By these words, Jesus is drawing us into a deeper symbolism that the wine will represent.

Jesus fills all six jars to the brim with water. John, the author of this book, is specific in his detail that the jars were for the purpose of Jewish purification. It was customary, by Jewish law, for hands to be ceremonially washed before meals, and the water from these jars made this possible. But by filling these jars with new water and up to the brim, Jesus is pointing us to a greater truth. In the Old Testament, wine was often used as a symbol of fulfillment. By replacing the water with new wine, Jesus was symbolizing the fulfillment of His coming. The empty jars represented the old Law, and the new jars full of wine represented the fulfillment of the Law through His life and sacrifice. Unlike ceremonial purification that temporarily provided cleansing, Jesus was bringing about a kind of purification that would overflow and never run dry. By His blood, Jesus would make a way for people to be eternally cleansed from their sins.

As the headwaiter tastes the new wine, he remarks to the bridegroom that unlike providing cheaper wine to his guests, the bridegroom has saved the fine wine until now. It was common for the bridegroom to serve his best wine first to his guests and the cheaper wine much later when his guests were satisfied enough not to notice it. The fine wine provided later in the ceremony is surprising to the headwaiter, but he does not realize who has brought this miracle. Jesus bringing the best wine symbolizes the superiority of His ministry. His message and ministry will bring lasting satisfaction.

This marriage celebration also points to the ultimate marriage celebration to come. Revelation 19:7 says, "Let us be glad, rejoice, and give him glory, because the marriage of the Lamb has come, and his bride has prepared herself." This passage speaks of the marriage supper of the Lamb when Christ as the bridegroom returns to bring His bride, the fellowship of believers, into eternity with Him. This wedding at Cana is only a mere glimpse of the ultimate wedding that is to come, where Jesus and His Church will be united forever. But for Jesus to make this union possible, He would have to sacrifice His own life. Unlike the bridegroom in this story, who struggled to make provision, Jesus would bring about ultimate provision by His death on the cross.

The first miracle that Jesus performs speaks volumes over the significance of His ministry. Like the newness of the wine, in His future death and resurrection, Christ will make all things new. Unlike the Law that could not provide forgiveness of sins, His blood would cleanse sinners' hearts and make them new. This wedding miracle causes us to rejoice over what Christ has done and prepares our hearts for the day in which we will participate in the ultimate wedding in which we will be united with Christ and met with abundance evermore.

> " **HIS MESSAGE AND MINISTRY WILL BRING LASTING SATISFACTION.**

day twelve questions

Read John 3:27-30. How are John the Baptist's words fulfilled in Christ?

John says this changing of water into wine is one of the first "signs" Jesus will do. Why do you think Jesus will use signs throughout His ministry? Consider the reaction of the disciples in John 2:11.

Read 2 Corinthians 5:17. How does the new coming from the old in the wine miracle speak to what happens for believers in this passage?

DAY 13

"
JESUS'S KINGDOM WAS THE BEGINNING OF A NEW HUMANITY THAT WOULD ALLOW HUMANKIND TO BE RESTORED TO A FLOURISHING LIFE IN GOD.

Beatitudes

READ MATTHEW 5:2-12

When Jesus begins His public ministry, He goes throughout all of Galilee, preaching the gospel and proclaiming that the kingdom of heaven has arrived. As the crowds become larger and larger, Jesus decides to pause on a mountain to preach His longest recorded sermon, the Sermon on the Mount.

As Jesus preaches the Sermon on the Mount, He overturns so much of who His disciples and the people of Israel thought the Messiah would be, and He tells them of His kingdom. And just like He is a Messiah, unlike the world, His kingdom is also an upside-down kingdom. His kingdom would not be for ruling over the nations. Instead, it would be for ruling over the hearts of those who believe in Him. Jesus's kingdom was the beginning of a new humanity that would allow humankind to be restored to a flourishing life in God.

Jesus begins His sermon by giving the Beatitudes. While it is common to hear the Beatitudes pulled apart or studied one at a time, it is wise to read and study them together. Jesus is crafting a sermon where each piece builds on the last. Many commentators have said that the first four beatitudes show the justification we receive from God, and the last four show the sanctification we receive from Him. Justification is when God declares us righteous because Christ's righteousness covers us through salvation. Sanctification is the ongoing process believers go through over the course of their lives as they walk with God and He conforms them to His image.

Jesus begins with the first beatitude: "Blessed are the poor in spirit, for the kingdom of heaven is theirs" (Matthew 5:3). This verse does not mean that those who are economically poor are blessed. Jesus is saying that those who recognize their spiritual lack and utter need before God will inherit the kingdom of heaven. When we realize there is nothing we can do to accomplish salvation, we understand the truth of the gospel.

Jesus goes on to the next beatitude: "Blessed are those who mourn for they will be comforted" (Matthew 5:4). Once we see our spiritual lack, we will mourn over our sin. We often like to overlook this and focus on the joy and forgiveness we have in Christ, but it is good to mourn the sin that the Lord mourns. We must see the destruction it wreaks on our souls so that we can thoroughly rejoice and be comforted in the gospel.

In verse 5, Jesus says, "Blessed are the humble, for they will inherit the earth" (Matthew 5:5). Once we see our need and are broken over sin, we will finally be willing to be humble before the Lord and recognize that He is God, and we are not. And when we willingly come under the Lord's authority, He places a desire within us to "hunger and thirst for righteousness" (Matthew 5:6). We begin to desire the things He desires because we have been united with Christ.

Jesus now moves into the four beatitudes that show the sanctification of believers or how they become more like Him. And fittingly, the first one is, "Blessed are the merciful, for they will be shown mercy" (Matthew 5:7). Jesus is the embodiment of mercy, and His coming to earth in and of itself shows the mercy of God to mankind. Because He is both God and man, Jesus understands the plight of sinners and sufferers, and He comes to rescue them. When we are aware of the depth of our sin and how Christ loves us and has shown us mercy by His death on the cross, we will desire to show mercy to others so that they may know Christ.

Jesus then says, "Blessed are the pure in heart for they will see God" (Matthew 5:8). Before we were saved, we were blind to sin and could not see God. He had to create new hearts within us so that we could understand the gospel. Being pure in heart is not something we could do on our own. As we grow in sanctification and have fellowship with Christ, our hearts are transformed and renewed to become more like His. The heart is used biblically to describe who we are. It goes beyond our feelings and emotions. Being "pure in heart" is another way of saying that God has become the anchor, focus, and desire of our entire beings.

The next beatitude is, "Blessed are the peacemakers, for they will be called sons of God" (Matthew 5:9). This might be one of the most revolutionary statements Jesus makes during His entire sermon. Many expected the Messiah to bring war and justice against Israel's enemies, but instead, He brings peace to mankind. God desires reconciliation with His chosen sons and daughters, and they will imitate His desire and participate in the "ministry of reconciliation" (2 Corinthians 5:18). The Christian enters the world to make peace with those who are enemies of God, but they will not always be readily welcomed. Jesus's last beatitude says this: "Blessed are those who are persecuted because of righteousness, for the kingdom of heaven is theirs" (Matthew 5:10). Even though the invitation to follow Jesus frees us from sin and gives us everlasting joy, it is not a guarantee to an easy life. In fact, the world will likely hate and persecute us at times because of our faith. We should expect the same treatment that our Savior received, and we can rejoice when we are faced with this persecution because He has called it a blessing.

We are exiles in this current world, awaiting our heavenly home, but Jesus has shown us through the Beatitudes how we can presently live our lives as citizens of His kingdom. Even though we are in the "already but not yet," we can anticipate the day that all of the redeemed will be reunited with our King, and we will perfectly express and experience the truth of the Beatitudes.

day thirteen questions

The last recorded time God spoke to His people on a mountain before the Sermon on the Mount was when His presence descended to Mt. Sinai to give the Law to Israel. Read about this in Exodus 19, and reflect on the differences between the setting of Mount Sinai and the setting of the Sermon on the Mount. What does this teach you about the Lord's presence with us?

How do the Beatitudes present a life contrary to a life lived for the world?

Why is it important to remember the gospel as you seek to live as a citizen of heaven? (Read Ephesians 2 to remind yourself of what Christ has done on your behalf.)

DAY 14

> WHAT AN INVITATION TO COME TO GOD IN PRAYER AS JESUS PRAYED, WITH OUTSTRETCHED HANDS AND FULL TRUST IN HIS CARE.

The Lord's Prayer

READ LUKE 11:1-4, MATTHEW 6:5-13

In Luke 11, we are introduced to Jesus praying alone, separated from His disciples. This was something Jesus often did—pulling away to pray and commune with His Father. Upon returning to the disciples, they eagerly insisted, "Lord, teach us to pray" (Luke 11:1). It was evident that Jesus was praying in such a way that challenged their understanding of prayer, and they humbled themselves to ask for instructions.

Jesus instructs them through the example of the Lord's Prayer. This prayer is one of the most recited and shared passages of Scripture among Christians. It has been held in reverence, rightfully so, since our Lord Jesus first spoke it. Jesus shared this rich prayer with His disciples as a means of teaching, correcting, and modeling to them the important elements of prayer. The Lord's Prayer includes six petitions. The first three requests are about God and His kingdom. We are called to pray for God's name to be honored, His kingdom to come, and His will to be done here on earth. The second three requests are about us. We are encouraged to ask for physical needs, relational needs, and spiritual needs.

In the book of Matthew, we find the Lord's Prayer in the middle of the Sermon on the Mount (Matthew 5-7). This sermon sets the tone that Jesus demands a righteousness that exceeds that of the scribes and the Pharisees. Jesus clarifies that He did not come for good appearances but to transform lives through the gospel. Jesus came to give us righteousness that works its way to our hearts and changes our attitudes.

As these teachings carried into the New Testament, Jesus saw that the Israelites viewed the Law in a ritualistic and habitual way. Instead, Jesus lays a foundational understanding of how the Law should be viewed (Matthew 5:17-20). The Law is the standard set before us by God to obey perfectly so that we might have a right relationship with Him. Evidenced in the history of Scripture, and even now, we do not perfectly obey. Therefore, Jesus came to make a way for us to have a right relationship with God. He came to fulfill the Law for all who would put their faith and trust in Him as their Savior. Because of this, God calls us to obey in response to our salvation, not as a means to earn a right standing with Him.

This teaching perfectly prefaces the Lord's prayer. There might be a temptation to approach prayer in a ritualistic or outwardly pleasing way, with the desires of our hearts and our attitude toward these practices unchanged. We might even pray without a true understanding of what our words mean or why we are even praying them. Therefore, Jesus provides a rich foundational theology for prayer by presenting the strong example of the Lord's Prayer amid His corrective teaching. He reminds His disciples of how we are to pray. No one is better able to teach us these valuable elements and the true nature of prayer than Jesus Himself.

Not only does Jesus teach us how to pray, but He ultimately gives us access to God in prayer. Jesus Christ made a way for us through salvation in Him to enter into the family of God, no longer orphans or strangers but as near as children to their fathers. It is only through the saving work of Christ that we are offered access to God in a personal and intimate way (John 14:6). In Christ, we gain access to God as His children. We are adopted as sons and daughters and possessing the title of heirs in Christ. In prayer, we have the opportunity to approach God as representatives of His family. What a gracious gift that we can address a holy God in such a relational and familial way.

The entirety of the Lord's Prayer models how we as Christians ought to approach a holy God—as needy creatures in need of grace—grace for daily bread, grace for forgiveness, grace for protection, and grace to behold the beauty of God's glory. As is the way for needy creatures, Christians ask, but our asking is always filled with hope. As Romans 8:32 reminds us, "He did not even spare his own Son but offered him up for us all. How will he not also with him grant us everything?" God, who offered up His own Son for our sake, will always graciously give His people all we need for life and godliness. He abounds in grace and overflows with care. What an invitation to come to God in prayer as Jesus prayed, with outstretched hands and full trust in His care.

> **JESUS CAME TO MAKE A WAY FOR US TO HAVE A RIGHT RELATIONSHIP WITH GOD.**

day fourteen questions

What did you learn from Jesus's model of the Lord's Prayer?
How does it lead you to assess your own prayer life?

Consider the reality that in Christ, we have gained access to approach a holy God.
How should you approach Him as such in prayer?

How can we depend on God's care for us in such a way that transforms our prayers and lives?

DAY 15

> WHEN WE REACH OUT FOR JESUS, HE DOES NOT RECOIL.

Jesus Heals the Leper

READ MARK 1:40-45

At the beginning of the book of Mark, a man with leprosy came to Jesus. It may be tempting to move quickly through a story like this one. A man came, he was sick, and he was healed. It is hard for our minds to fathom what that would have been like, so we move on. But before we continue too quickly, let us consider that this brief exchange would have been incredibly controversial.

Leprosy was a very contagious skin disease that led to the deterioration of the skin. In the Old Testament, someone with a skin disease must "have his clothes torn and his hair hanging loose, and he must cover his mouth and cry out, 'Unclean, unclean!' He will remain unclean as long as he has the disease; he is unclean. He must live alone in a place outside the camp" (Leviticus 13:45-46). He was to live separately and alone, apart from others, because he was unclean. He was not included in the community or able to work his normal occupation. He was unable to touch others. A husband was excluded from his family and unable to kiss his wife. A mother was separated from her children to keep the children safe from disease. To have leprosy was a lonely and painful affair.

Not only this but in the Old Testament, leprosy was generally regarded as divine punishment. For example, when Mariam spoke against Moses in the wilderness, she was turned temporarily into a leper (Numbers 12:10). And later in the Bible, we learn that when the greedy servant Gehazi took a devious bribe, he was cursed with leprosy as his punishment (2 Kings 5:20-27). Indeed the root verb for leprosy in Hebrew means "to smite," hence Old Testament Jews often viewed leprosy as a divine judgment from God.

Within the context of this book, the leper broke the Levitical law that required him to be distanced from others. He came and fell on his knees before Jesus, pleading, "If you are willing, you can make me clean!" (Mark 1:40). This leper defied cultural, societal, and religious norms to beg before Jesus, his very presence endangering those around him who could also become sick. If this act of desperation failed, he could be punished by the religious leaders. But he was willing to take the risk.

When face to face with the leper, Jesus did not recoil. He did not pull back from the scabs or protect Himself from disease. He did not condemn the man for his filth. Instead, He "had compassion" on him. Jesus touched the man, likely the first touch the leper experienced since contracting the disease. And the man was instantly healed.

Often, when we feel dirty—whether because of a sin we have committed or one that has been committed against us—we pull away from God. We feel ugly and unworthy. We recoil at our filth in shame. We think that surely such a good and holy God would never want to associate with someone like us. Like a rich man who sneers at the poor, we view God in white robes, unwilling to touch our dirty scabs, lest we somehow pollute His divine perfection.

To be fair, that is how the world usually works. If a young child with dirty, muddy hands touches a brand new, white shirt, we all know what happens. Their dirt is transferred. Dirtiness pollutes. But amazingly, with Jesus, something different happens. Instead of the leper making Jesus unclean, Jesus made the leper clean. He healed the man with a touch because His power and purity were greater than the man's disease. His goodness was so secure that He was able to touch such filth and not be tainted by it.

The story of the leper is not unique in the New Testament. Throughout His ministry, Jesus continued to heal the dirty and the broken because that is who He is. Today still, He offers healing and forgiveness, cleanliness, and community to all who would come to Him. This can be our story, too, for Scripture promises that all who trust in Jesus will be made clean. On the cross, Jesus took upon Himself all of our dirt, sin, and brokenness and destroyed its power. In His resurrection, He offers us new life, granting us His perfect righteousness in place of our sin.

So to the one feeling dirty, run to Jesus. To the one who feels unworthy, run to the One who is full of compassion. When we reach out for Jesus, He does not recoil. Instead, He pulls us close, cleansing us and making us white as snow. He removes our guilt and our shame and restores us to Himself.

> " **INSTEAD OF THE LEPER MAKING JESUS UNCLEAN, JESUS MADE THE LEPER CLEAN.**

day fifteen questions

What sins, behaviors, or circumstances have kept you from running boldly to the Lord?

Read 1 John 1:9. In light of God's great mercy and eagerness to forgive, spend time confessing specific sins to the Lord.

Read Luke 8:43-48. What similarities do you notice between this story and the story of the leper?

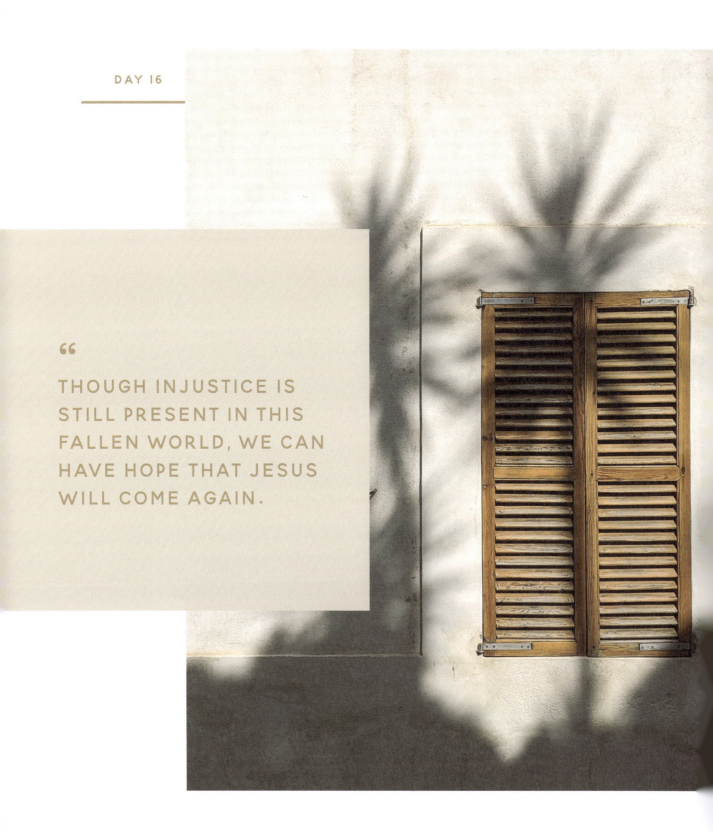

DAY 16

> "Though injustice is still present in this fallen world, we can have hope that Jesus will come again.

The Coming One

READ MATTHEW 11:2-19, LUKE 7:18-35

According to Matthew 14:1-5, John the Baptist was in prison for calling out the corruption among the Roman leaders who had authority over the Jewish people. The ruler of Galilee, Herod Antipas, had unlawfully married his brother's wife, Herodias, and John confronted Herod about his sin. As a result, Herod wanted to kill John, but fearing how the Jewish people would react, he threw him in prison. A prophet, John, was sent by God to preach about repentance and prepare a people for Jesus's coming. During his preaching, John called out the sin of the Pharisees, the proud religious authorities, and called for them to be humble. He told them they would be cut off from the covenant community because of their wickedness and stubbornness (Matthew 3:10). Based on Scripture, John believed that the Coming One, the Savior of the world, would enact divine justice against evildoers and the unjust. John pointed to Jesus as this Judge and Redeemer to restore God's good and righteous kingdom. But, as he sat in prison, he was overcome with doubt. *Perhaps Jesus was not the One. Could there be someone else coming?*

John's circumstances affected his faith, and he became discouraged. But when Jesus heard of John's questions, He did not criticize or condemn John for his doubt. Jesus understood that the fallenness of the world is trying, and His people were weak. Jesus sent a report of encouragement and correction to John. He wanted John to know that "the blind receive their sight, the lame walk, those with leprosy are cleansed, the deaf hear, the dead are raised, and the poor are told the good news" (Matthew 11:5). Jesus was working to relieve suffering among God's people to prove that He was truly the Son of God. He fulfilled the words of the Old Testament prophet Isaiah. Isaiah foreshadowed Jesus's day of redemption when he said, "Then the eyes of the blind will be opened, and the ears of the deaf unstopped. Then the lame will leap like a deer, and the tongue of the mute will sing for joy, for water will gush in the wilderness, and streams in the desert" (Isaiah 35:5-6). Jesus's first coming brought restoration and life to God's people. He came to bless rather than to condemn. Instead of judging, He took on judgment to satisfy the wrath of God and pay for sin. Divine justice would surely be settled, but it would be through Jesus's suffering and death on a cross.

Hearing that their prophet was doubting led John's followers to question as well. Jesus turned to the crowd and assured them that John was the prophet who came in the spirit of Elijah and prepared a way for the Lord (Malachi 4:5-6). The book of Luke's account of Jesus's message exposes who responded with faith and who did not. Those who had been a part of John's baptism ministry had readied hearts to trust in "God's way of righteousness" (Luke 7:29). Tax collectors, seen as traitors among the Jewish people, were in this group. Belittled and rejected by society, the tax collectors were repentant of their sin and knew they needed a Savior.

On the other hand, the Pharisees and the Law scholars, who John did not baptize, did not respond well to Jesus's message. They hardened their hearts, ignored their sin, and refused to see their need for Jesus. As a result, Jesus likened them to bad-tempered children who throw fits when their playmates do not follow in their ways. Similarly, the Pharisees thought their religious scholarship made them superior, and they stewed in anger when Jesus and John pointed out otherwise. They did not have the faith to truly mourn their sin with the prophet John and celebrate their redemption with King Jesus.

Through the report brought to him in prison, John indeed witnessed Jesus, the Coming One, coming to him as the Word of God. Though he was still physically chained, he received a message of hope and victory that set him free spiritually: God was still working to restore His world, forgive sin, and defeat evil. Jesus explained to the crowd that though John was a great servant, those who would see the full revelation of God's kingdom were greater. Future believers would be greater not because of ministry success or merit but because of what they would witness. John did not see the total picture of Christ's saving work, but today, we who are believers in Jesus do.

By the Holy Spirit and the revelation in Scripture, we discover the complete accomplishment of God's plan of redemption: Jesus's life, death, resurrection, and ascension to His heavenly throne. Knowing this truth encourages us in hard times. We know how the story ends. Jesus conquered evil and sin. Though injustice is still present in this fallen world, we can have hope that Jesus will come again. And when He returns, Jesus will judge the wicked and carry out the divine justice of which John spoke.

> " **JESUS WAS WORKING TO RELIEVE SUFFERING AMONG GOD'S PEOPLE TO PROVE THAT HE WAS TRULY THE SON OF GOD.**

day sixteen questions

How do you react when God acts in ways that are contrary to your expectations?

How do the different ministries of John and Jesus work together toward God's plan of redemption?

How can we be children of a "responsive generation"? During times of challenge and uncertainty, in what ways can believers show a faithful response to the gospel?

Reflection

REVIEW ALL PASSAGES FROM THE LAST 6 DAYS

Summarize the main points from this week's Scripture readings.

What did you observe from this week's passages about the life of Jesus and His character?

What do this week's passages reveal about the condition of mankind and yourself?

How do these passages point to the gospel?

How should you respond to these Scriptures? What specific action steps can you take this week to apply them in your life?

Write a prayer in response to your study of God's Word. Adore God for who He is, confess sins He revealed in your own life, ask Him to empower you to walk in obedience, and pray for anyone who comes to mind as you study.

DAY 17

> IN JESUS, WE CAN PARTAKE OF HIS ABUNDANT GRACE AND BE SATISFIED BY HIS WISDOM.

Jesus Carries Our Burdens

READ MATTHEW 11:28-30

Jesus's declaration to relieve the burdens of His people came after the encounter that we read about in last week's commentary on Matthew 11:2-19. Jesus pointed out the lack of wisdom of the Pharisees and Law scholars and their misplaced trust in their own knowledge and abilities. In Matthew 11:20-24, He continued to preach to them about their lack of faith toward the miracles of God. During His ministry so far, Jesus had healed the sick and calmed a storm, proving that He was the Son of God. Jesus called out cities like Chorazin and Bethsaida, which were places where He performed these miracles. Though the residents saw the works of God, they did not repent and believe in Christ. Jesus compared these places to Tyre, Sidon, and Sodom, which were notorious for pagan worship and moral corruption. But, Jesus claimed that if the wicked had seen the miracles like the Pharisees and the Law scholars have witnessed, the people of Tyre, Sidon, and Sodom would have repented. Tyre, Sidon, and Sodom were symbols for the lowly and contrite—those who did not take pride in their own merits of righteousness. This humility is the basis for true wisdom, which the "wise and intelligent" (Matthew 11:25) of a wayward culture refuses. God is the giver of true wisdom, and according to His divine will, He reveals it to those who come before Him humbly through Jesus Christ.

Jesus begins Matthew 11:28 by saying, "Come to me." Scholars note that this invitation mirrors the call of Wisdom in Proverbs 9:5. There, Wisdom is personified as the great possessor of truth who wants to give it generously. Wisdom sets her table with an abundance of food and welcomes the lonely traveler to partake. Through this invitation, Jesus stood in Wisdom's place and claimed to be its true source and giver. He directed this invitation to those "weary and burdened" (Matthew 11:28). When the humble crowd heard this statement, they might have thought of Jeremiah 31:25, which states, "I satisfy the thirsty person and feed all those who are weak." These words refer to God promising to return the Israelites from exile. With their kingdom destroyed, the Israelites were lost, wandering in a foreign land, hungry, and parched. God promised to lead them back to the Promised Land and give them rest from their enemies. But, this state of exile was a picture of those who were truly lost in sin. Jesus claimed to fulfill God's promise of restoration by giving nourishment to the spiritually weak. The Promised Land symbolized the presence and blessing of God and rest from the burden of sin. This rest comes from Jesus alone; it is not the result of merit or inner strength.

Jesus then gave the command, "Take up my yoke and learn from me" (Matthew 11:29). A yoke is a wooden cross piece placed on the necks of animals or people when pulling farming equipment. The yoke was indicative of heavy labor and symbolized slavery. The humble crowd carried the yoke of sin. They were burdened by the fallen nature of humanity and their inability to please God. They mourned the rebellion, sickness, and evil present in their hearts as well as in the world. The Pharisees and the lawmakers carried the yoke of earning their own righteousness. They were slaves to the Law and worked to no end to earn good standing. Through their dependence on the Law, they were also arrogant and only focused on outward appearances. Jesus flipped this imagery of a yoke upside down and claimed, "My yoke is easy and my burden is light" (Matthew 11:30). God in the flesh, Jesus was the perfect human being. Without sin, He obtained righteousness. By His life, death, and resurrection, Jesus won for His people the blessing of rest in the presence of God. His righteousness is the yoke that He gives to His people, as He invites them to humbly lay down their own hearts at His table of wisdom.

As we consider our own burdens and feelings of loneliness, discouragement, worry, concern, let us remember that Jesus offers us rest. He provides those who are believers in Him with relief. This rest starts with humility and true wisdom. We must recognize that we are sinners, wandering exiles away from home and in dire need of sustenance. We must see our need for Jesus and heed His invitation. We can leave our self-made yokes at the door and approach His table with peace, knowing that Jesus took our cares to the cross and died for them. In Jesus, we can partake of His abundant grace and be satisfied by His wisdom. This wisdom gives us an eternal perspective that fixes our gazes above our trying circumstances and reminds us of our identity in God. Though this world will continue to make us weary, may we continue to hold to Jesus's righteousness—His yoke—for the sake of our souls.

> " BY HIS LIFE, DEATH, AND RESURRECTION, JESUS WON FOR HIS PEOPLE THE BLESSING OF REST IN THE PRESENCE OF GOD.

day seventeen questions

Read Philippians 2:5-8. Describe how Jesus demonstrated utmost humility.

Identify things that may be keeping you from laying down your burdens before Christ. Write out a prayer, asking for help in overcoming these obstacles.

How can you imitate the humility of Christ?

DAY 18

> "JESUS IS THIS SOWER WHO SOWS THE SEED OF THE GOSPEL BY GIVING THE WORD OF GOD TO THE PEOPLE.

The Parable of the Sower

READ MATTHEW 13:1-23

The parable of the sower is one of the most famous parables Jesus gave in His ministry. It is the first in an extensive series of parables that Jesus gives while sitting in a boat on the Sea of Galilee with a large crowd standing on the shore. Parables are short stories that contain spiritual truths for the listener. When Jesus gives the parable of the sower, His disciples do not understand why He chooses to teach through story. He is the Son of God and the Messiah—why does He not speak directly? Would that not allow more people to understand and follow Him?

One of the most common phrases Jesus will say after He gives a parable is: "Let anyone who has ears listen" (Matthew 13:9). Jesus teaches in parables to reveal to a person if they can hear and understand the truth of the gospel. Those who have "ears" that are spiritually sensitive to the kingdom of heaven will ponder the parables of Christ and see the wisdom of God. Those with hardened hearts against Christ will be confused and stumble over parables. In essence, parables reveal the judgment of the Lord against those who reject His Word.

Jesus tells His disciples that the fact that there are people who do not understand His parables fulfills Isaiah's prophecy of the people of Israel (Isaiah 6:9-10). They have become cold-hearted toward the Lord and cannot see or hear the truth of the gospel. But He says that the people who have eyes and ears that are opened to truth are blessed. What they see and hear as Jesus teaches is the fulfillment of what the prophets proclaimed. The prophets of the Old Testament longed to see the redemptive work of God come to fruition, and the people who stood before Jesus as He taught on the Sea of Galilee were seeing just that! Followers of Christ today have access to the completed canon of Scripture, which contains the breathtaking story of redemption in its entirety. The prophets and the people on the shores of Galilee would have longed to hold the Bibles that sit near us today.

After Jesus explains the purpose of parables to His disciples, He addresses the meaning behind the parable of the sower. In the parable of the sower, there is a farmer who sows seeds, and the seeds fall on different kinds of soil. The soil the seed falls on determines how it will grow, if it grows at all. Jesus is this Sower who sows the seed of the gospel by giving the Word of God to the people. How people receive His Word can be compared to how the soil receives the seed.

The good news of the kingdom of God is like a seed. While the seed does not seem to change the ground it is planted in at first, it produces life and nutrients in the unseen depths of the earth. As the truth of Jesus's kingdom takes root in our hearts, it produces more change than any kingdom of the world could ever dream!

Three of the soils that the sower's seed falls on come as warnings to those who hear and receive the gospel. The first scenario Jesus uses as a warning is a seed that falls on a path and not in the soil. This represents those who hear the good news of Christ but never allow it to enter their hearts. When people are not affected by the truth of the Word of God, Satan easily snatches it away and deceives them into thinking it is unneeded—that the things they know about the gospel are purely intellectual. The good news of the kingdom of God has never changed their life.

The second scenario depicts a seed that falls on rocky ground. While the seed appears to enter the ground, it never takes root and eventually dies. Jesus uses this seed to describe those who have emotional responses to the gospel and appear to accept it with joy. We think that these people are believers, but they fall away from the faith when hardship and persecution come. It was never faith to begin with; it was only joy in the blessings they could potentially receive from Christ. When the false expectations of carefree and painless lives in Christ are shattered, they turn from Him and search for it elsewhere.

The third scenario depicts a seed that enters the ground but is choked by thorns. The people who represent this seed hear the gospel and believe it, but they have divided hearts. While they recognize the truth, they are unfruitful because they are consumed with things of the world. They know the truth, but they do not live in the freedom the Lord offers them. But the last soil is the kind that is good ground in which seed can thrive. This soil represents those who eagerly receive the gospel, and because the Lord has softened their hearts to know the truth, they seek the Lord, and He conforms them to His image. They produce abundant fruit because of their union with Christ.

If we believe in Jesus, we will fall into one of these last two categories of soil. The seed of the gospel has not just fallen on the path, it has taken root in our hearts. And we did not accept Jesus because of strong emotion or a desire for a blessing but because we desired Him and saw Him as true joy and satisfaction. However, we must be careful not to let the thorns of the world choke out the truth of the gospel. All of us, in one way or another, deal with the thorns of the world, but if we remain in Christ, He will help us uproot them and grow in Him.

Do we have ears that listen to His truth? We will hear Jesus as He beckons us to let Him weed out the thorns of the world so our lives can be fruitful in Him. We, like the soil, cannot change on our own. Rather, we must be tended by the Sower of the gospel, our faithful Savior above.

day eighteen questions

How would parables have frustrated those who hated Jesus and rejected Him, especially the religious leaders of Israel, as He taught on the Sea of Galilee? How would parables have blessed those who believed Him?

In the parable of the sower, Jesus compares His good news to a seed. From knowing what seeds do and how human beings rely on them, what truths does this show you about the power of the gospel?

How might you be like the soil choked by thorns? Write a prayer, asking the Lord to uproot any thorns of the world in your heart so that you may grow and bear abundant fruit in Him.

DAY 19

> JESUS IS COMPASSIONATE TOWARD US, AND HE INVITES US INTO HIS FAMILY.

Unbelief in His Hometown

READ LUKE 4:16-30

Many of us may remember the first extended trips we took away from home. Perhaps those trips included leaving for college and returning home for Christmas break. Or perhaps they were trips spending the night with family out of town or at summer camp. Maybe some of us can remember the eager anticipation of sleeping in our own beds again, seeing family and friends, and visiting our favorite restaurants. Or maybe your memories of "home" are painful. Perhaps you identify more with Jesus in today's reading. In today's reading, Jesus took a trip back home after a successful time in Capernaum, but His trip was not quite so pleasant. Though others around Israel began revering Jesus, those in His hometown did not view Him quite so highly.

When Jesus went home in Luke 4, He visited the synagogue on the Sabbath as was His tradition. During the service, He stood up to read from the scroll with all eyes fixed on Him. He found the words of Isaiah 61, which spoke of good news for the poor, and the eyes of the blind being opened. As He finished, He closed the scroll and proclaimed, "This Scripture has been fulfilled" (Luke 4:21). The people listening were amazed and wondered at His gracious words, but they also scoffed. "Isn't this Joseph's son?" they asked.

Unbeknownst to them, Jesus was the fulfillment of these Old Testament prophecies. He is the Promised One and the source of redemption. He cares for the poor and binds up their wounds. He opens the eyes of the blind. He wants all to come to Him and be fed with the bread of life. Just as Isaiah 61 promises, Jesus would bring freedom for the prisoners and liberty for the oppressed. In reading these verses, Jesus was offering His family and friends insight into His mission. But just like Elijah and Elisha, God would use Jesus to bring freedom to the Gentiles (Luke 4:25-27). And the Jews in Jesus's hometown did not like that.

Jesus knew their thoughts, perceiving their objections and questions. He knew that they would reject Him, just as the prophets of the Old Testament were rejected in their hometowns. Though these men and women had likely watched Jesus grow up, observing His good character, grace, and love, they quickly turned on Him. His words at the synagogue angered them so much that they wanted to kill Him. They tried to throw Him off a cliff, but He was able to escape unharmed.

Perhaps many of us can identify with Jesus's story. Family can be difficult to love. It can be lonely to be the only Christian in a family. Perhaps holiday visits with family feel like going to war. Or it may feel impossible to speak kindly, love well, and maintain patience amid family chaos. Sometimes it can feel as if all our siblings want to do is trip us up or make us sin. Perhaps they want us to revert to old patterns of behavior to prove that we are not better than them and that God has not changed us that much.

Or perhaps it is in our workplaces where we are rejected for following Christ. If we do not manipulate the numbers to make the team look better, we will not get the promotion. Or if we do not join in the office gossip, we will become the office gossip. Jesus understands. He, too, was rejected by His family and friends, though He was pure without blemish. Jesus was the only perfect One, full of infinite love, grace, and mercy, but He was betrayed by those closest to Him. Because of this, we are also rejected by the world. However, Jesus is compassionate toward us, and He invites us into His family. As we repent and turn to Him, He has the power to turn us from enemies of God into His friends.

Jesus did not have the warm welcome back that many would expect. His friends and family did not throw Him a banquet or treat Him with special respect. Instead, they questioned Him: Who is this? Do we not know Him? Why does He think He is so special? Yet, while His hometown would reject Him, others would gladly receive Him. Through repentance and faith, we can be united with Him, adopted into His family, and called sons and daughters of the King. His opinion is the one that should matter most to us. He is the longing of our souls and will one day return to make all things new. And when He returns, He will throw an extravagant feast and celebrate all who are His, as we come home to Him into glory.

> " THROUGH REPENTANCE AND FAITH, WE CAN BE UNITED WITH HIM, ADOPTED INTO HIS FAMILY, AND CALLED SONS AND DAUGHTERS OF THE KING.

day nineteen questions

Why did the people in His hometown reject Jesus?

What are some ways that we can respond to the truth of God's Word? Think of examples in your life when you have either rejected or been open to biblical truths.

Spend time asking the Lord to reveal areas of hidden doubt and spiritual hardness in your heart. Repent and receive His grace afresh today.

DAY 20

> THE GLORY OF THE GOSPEL MUST NOT FADE SO MUCH IN OUR LIVES THAT IT CAUSES US TO BE COMPLACENT IN KEEPING IT TO OURSELVES.

Jesus and Nicodemas

READ JOHN 3:1-17

John 3 opens with a man approaching Jesus at night. His name is Nicodemus, a Pharisee and a member of the Sanhedrin, the supreme Jewish ruling council. As an esteemed Pharisee, Nicodemus was a prominent teacher of the Law who taught strict adherence to its rules. And as inconspicuous as this meeting with Jesus may appear, Nicodemus is committing a brave act by approaching Him, as the Sanhedrin were the ones who plotted to kill Jesus (John 11:47-57). Therefore, they would not have approved of Nicodemus approaching Jesus to ask genuine questions about who He is.

When Nicodemus approaches Jesus, he calls Jesus "Rabbi," which means "teacher." Then he makes the statement, "Rabbi, we know that you are a teacher who has come from God, for no one could perform these signs you do unless God were within him" (John 3:2). Even though Nicodemus acknowledges that Jesus has come from God, he sees him more as a moral teacher with spiritual gifts than God in the flesh. He believes that Jesus's signs point to a sense of spiritual authority, but his coming to Jesus is perhaps more about curiosity about his teachings than belief in them. Jesus answers Nicodemus's statement by telling him that no one can enter into the kingdom of God unless born again. Thinking that Jesus meant physical birth, Nicodemus is confused, for it is not humanly possible for a grown adult to return to his mother's womb and be born again. But Nicodemus was confusing a spiritual reality with a physical one.

Jesus explains that to enter into the kingdom of God, he must be born of water and spirit. "Water" and "spirit" were words that Nicodemus would recognize in reading the Old Testament. The term "spirit" was used in the Old Testament to describe God's presence to bring about blessing and righteousness. For example, the prophet Joel prophesied of the coming day when God would pour out His Spirit on humanity. The term "water" was used figuratively in the Old Testament to describe renewal or cleansing. Often, prophets would use both words together to communicate deep spiritual renewal that came from God (Ezekiel 36:25-26). By using the words "water" and "spirit," Jesus describes the way for true salvation. Nicodemus believed that as a Jew, he earned entrance into the kingdom of God. But

Jesus is teaching the opposite—that is, it is only by the inward cleansing of the heart from sin brought about by the Holy Spirit that someone is saved and brought into God's kingdom.

To further explain this, Jesus uses earthly examples. First, he contrasts physical and spiritual birth. Unlike physical birth, which produces physical life, the new birth brought about by the Holy Spirit produces spiritual life. Second, just like the wind cannot be seen or controlled, we can still see evidence of its presence, so the Holy Spirit's work of transformation cannot be controlled or physically seen, but the evidence of spiritual renewal a person can.

However, Nicodemus does not understand how inward transformation is brought about by salvation. As a Pharisee, he was confident that because of his obedience to the Law, he did not need to be born again. But Nicodemus was missing the process of regeneration, which is when God transforms a heart as it is cleansed from sin. This causes a new birth in which a believer's old life is gone, and a new life begins. This new birth is not caused by perfect works or obedience to rules. It is only done by the work of the Holy Spirit and belief in Jesus Christ.

Verses 16-17 explain the glorious truth of the gospel. First, they show us the love of God. Verse 16 tells us that God so loved the world that He gave His One and only Son. God did not bring about a way of salvation out of a sense of obligation but deep desire. It was from the depths of His great love that He sent His Son to die for us. His decision to bring Jesus for salvation and not condemnation also speaks to His love. His heart desired to bring salvation for the sins of people, not condemnation for their sins. Second, they show us the way of salvation. Verse 16 says that those who believe in Jesus are rescued from the punishment of sin, eternal separation from God. They will not perish in separation from Him but will have life in Him and with Him forever.

As we read more of Nicodemus's story in other parts of Scripture, we learn that though Nicodemus struggled with the truth that Jesus shared, his character continued to develop in a beautiful way through the teaching of Christ. After the crucifixion, it was Nicodemus who provided the embalming spices for Jesus, suggesting his relationship had indeed developed with His Savior. And in John 7, he goes against the Sanhedrin and argues that Jesus should at least be heard.

The entrance into the kingdom of God and the new birth Jesus is speaking of is only made possible by the saving work of Christ on the cross and faith in Him. At this point in Nicodemus's story, he believed that salvation came from works of the Law and his social status seemed to darken his understanding of the truth of salvation. He could not see that Jesus was telling him that salvation would come through Him. We read of this and are reminded of this reality today. So many people are walking in spiritual darkness, completely blinded to the truth of the gospel. Maybe like Nicodemus, they falsely believe that their good works are what saves them. This is why the gospel is so important. As believers, we have been brought from death to life and should desire this for others. The glory of the gospel must not fade so much in our lives that it causes us to be complacent in keeping it to ourselves. We have a message of salvation to share as we partner with the Holy Spirit to bring people out of darkness into His marvelous light.

day twenty questions

Nicodemus knew that there was something special about Jesus but did not yet believe His teachings. What is the difference between knowing Jesus and knowing about Jesus?

Read Titus 3:5. In light of this passage and today's reading, what truths are essential in our understanding of the gospel?

How can you guard yourself against trying to earn or maintain your salvation by your works?

DAY 21

> HE IS IN THE BUSINESS OF REDEEMING AND WILL NEVER TURN AWAY ANYONE WHO SEARCHES FOR IT.

Jesus and the Woman at the Well

READ JOHN 4

In John 4, we are introduced to Jesus's encounter of the woman at the well. This interaction stands as one of the longest documented conversations between Jesus and any other individual in the gospels. The woman is never named, but we learn quite a lot about her. She was a woman living during a time when women were disregarded, and Samaritans were a race despised by the Jews. She was presently unmarried but had been married many times before. She was of no social regard, nor did she have anything to bring to Jesus. Yet, Jesus took lengths of time to speak with her.

The story begins when Jesus was traveling to Galilee and passed through Samaria to take a break in the town of Sychar. His disciples had gone to retrieve food, and Jesus sat down at a well to rest around noon. He noticed a Samaritan woman coming to get water from the well. Culturally, it was custom for women to go in pairs in the mornings to draw water together, making it somewhat of a social occasion. But because the woman came alone at midday, we can infer that she was likely an outcast. Instead of looking past her like many would, Jesus asked her for a drink of water. The Samaritan woman responded by pointing out the socially obvious fact that Jews did not associate with Samaritans: "How is it that you, a Jew, ask for a drink from me, a Samaritan woman?" (John 4:9). Jesus's response pointed beyond a simple drink of water and provoked her to consider the person to whom she was really speaking. Again, she posed more questions, wondering how someone could make such claims about themselves, "You aren't greater than our father Jacob, are you?" (John 4:12). Jesus could have easily explained that He was much greater than Jacob, but instead, He provided a metaphor. "Everyone who drinks from this water will get thirsty again, but whoever drinks from the water I will give him will never get thirsty again. In fact, the water I will give him will become a well of water springing up in him for eternal life" (John 4:13-14). He compared the water in the well to Himself, the living water, which was not even truly a comparison. One will run dry, but One will last forever. This tangible example provided a gospel presentation to the woman. Jesus was inviting her to find true and lasting fulfillment in Him.

Jesus knew the woman well and recounted her marriages and her current whereabouts. She obviously was surprised by His truthful claims and, in turn, decided Jesus must have been a prophet. She goes on to talk about her place of worship versus the Jews' place of worship. But she was missing the point. Jesus was not concerned with her place of worship but who she worshiped. He spoke of the coming Messiah, the One who comes to take away the sins of the world and unite worshipers of God together in Spirit and Truth. He is the One who offers us a drink that will never run dry, who replenishes our thirst and brings us fulfillment and satisfaction in this life and the next. Upon hearing the message of the Messiah, the woman expressed belief in the One who was to come, unaware that He stood before her. Then Jesus astounded her with His declaration, "I, the one speaking to you, am he" (John 4:26).

This story reveals the nature of Jesus as compassionate and loving as He crosses social and racial lines to come near to someone many pushed away. It tells us of His thoughtfulness and intentionality as He recounts the woman's life and offers that which is eternal over that which is temporal through the hope of the gospel. This story tells us how accessible Jesus is to us. He required nothing of the Samaritan woman but offered the message of the gospel freely and generously. She did not need wealth or status to receive life in Christ. All that was required was that she repented and received the news of Jesus Christ. Jesus is not simple, but His message is.

The story of Jesus and the woman at the well brings hope to us, too. In John 7:37-38, Jesus speaks to the crowd before His crucifixion, "If anyone is thirsty, let him come to me and drink." The invitation is not only extended to the women at the well but anyone who finds themselves outcast, ignored, depleted by their efforts, suffering, broken, or longing for more. Jesus opens the invitation to anyone who will come, repent, and put their faith in Him. He is in the business of redeeming and will never turn away anyone who searches for it.

For those of us who are in Christ, we can share in the joy of the Samaritan woman when she realized what happened. The delight and hope she found in knowing Jesus could not be contained. She immediately left the encounter to share all that she had seen and heard with the people in the town. Her testimony brought many to believe and piqued the curiosity of some, so when Jesus came, many gathered to hear from Him. Upon His departure, the Samaritans said, "We no longer believe because of what you said, since we have heard for ourselves and know that this really is the Savior of the world" (John 4:42). The woman could have never known the events that would take place that day, but a small conversation changed her life and the life of many others forever. May we too rest in the true hope we find in Jesus and be quick to share it with all who will listen.

day twenty-one questions

In what ways do you connect with the story of Jesus and the woman at the well? What do you learn about the character of Jesus by studying His interactions with the Samaritan woman?

What can we learn from the response of the Samaritan woman after she spoke with Jesus?

Who in your life might be an outcast or ignored? How can you seek out to share the hope of Jesus with them? Spend time specifically praying for opportunities.

DAY 22

> AS WE DWELL ON THE GREATNESS OF GOD, WE WILL FIND OURSELVES PREPARED TO WALK THROUGH THE HARD THINGS OF LIFE.

Walking on Water

READ MATTHEW 14:22-33

It was the end of the day, and Jesus ushered His disciples to go on out ahead of Him in a boat. After dismissing the crowd gathered to see Him, He went off by Himself to pray to the Lord. As the disciples waited for Him, a storm developed on the sea. The sea waves rocked the ship violently as the wind and pelting rain rattled the boat. Then, in the fourth watch of the night, when the disciples had been vigilantly battling the storm for nearly nine hours, they noticed a figure on the water.

Not knowing who it could be, the disciples believed the figure was a ghost, and they cried out in fear. But He was not a ghost—it was Jesus. He called out to them, "It is I, don't be afraid." By using this phrase, Jesus's words connect to God's words in the Old Testament. This is because the work for "I" here is the Greek word *eimi*, which means "I exist, I am." And when God would reveal Himself to His people, He would often do so by describing Himself as "I am." It was an expression that communicated the deity of God and His holiness. So as Jesus called out to His disciples, He was not simply letting them know it was Him; He was confirming His deity—the God of the universe walking toward them on the waves, and because it was the great I am, there was no reason to fear.

Even though Jesus identified Himself, there was still some hesitancy amongst the disciples. Peter asked Jesus to call him out on the waters if it was really Him. Jesus beckoned for Peter to come, and Peter stepped out of the rocking boat and unto the turbulent sea. For Peter to make such an effort amongst the storm shows that Peter had faith. The voice of His Lord called Him out onto the sea he had been battling, and Peter started out toward Him. However, Peter's faith faltered as he took his eyes off Jesus and looked at the storm around him. As he noticed the howling wind and the spraying waters around his feet, he became afraid, causing his legs to begin to sink. He cried out for Jesus to save him, and immediately Jesus grabbed

Peter's hand and brought him up out of the waters, all the while saying to him, "You of little faith, why did you doubt?" (Matthew 14:31).

Peter's reaction to the storm around him revealed that he doubted the One to whom he was walking. His faith in Jesus kept him afloat as He walked on water, but once he took his eyes off Christ, he began to sink. At that moment, Peter forgot the greatness of the Lord, viewing the storm as greater. Jesus's words to him are not condemning Peter for not having any faith, but He is saying his faith is small. His question "why did you doubt?" reveals Peter did not need to doubt. Peter had forgotten that the One who called him out on the water was the Lord over all creation. The God who created the waves and commanded them was before him, but Peter allowed the storm around him to distract him from this truth.

When Peter and Jesus came into the boat, the stormy winds ceased, and the disciples worshiped Jesus, acknowledging His glory and Lordship. Their response was right, as God deserves to be worshiped for who He is. However, it was not until after the storm stopped and they recognized Jesus on the water that they worshiped Him. If they truly trusted Jesus, they would have worshiped Him during the storm, not after. Like Peter, their faith was small. Jesus would have to keep showing His glory to them again and again for their faith to grow.

Often, this passage of Scripture is interpreted to encourage believers to have faith in the storms of life. While this is a helpful sentiment and a good principle to follow, this passage speaks less about our circumstances and more about the God who controls them. Just like Jesus controlled the wind and the waves, so does He control our circumstances. We miss His glory and allow ourselves to be shaken by fear when we keep our eyes on what is around us instead of on Him. Like Peter, we can feel as if our faith is small. But even if we do feel as if our faith is small, we should not be discouraged by this but seek to see God as greater in our lives. As we fixate on the truth of who God is and worship Him in all circumstances, He will be bigger than the things of this life that tear our attention away from Him. As we dwell on the greatness of God, we will find ourselves prepared to walk through the hard things of life. Our doubts and fears fade when we trust in the One who holds the universe in His hands. He is a God who is greater than anything we face.

> **JUST LIKE JESUS CONTROLLED THE WIND AND THE WAVES, SO DOES HE CONTROL OUR CIRCUMSTANCES.**

day twenty-two questions

Read Matthew 8:24-27. How do you see similarities between this passage to today's text? What do you learn about Jesus?

How does worship impact our faith?

Why is it easy to forget who God is when we are afraid? What truths about God can you focus on when you are afraid?

Reflection
REVIEW ALL PASSAGES FROM THE LAST 6 DAYS

Summarize the main points from this week's Scripture readings.

What did you observe from this week's passages about the life of Jesus and His character?

What do this week's passages reveal about the condition of mankind and yourself?

How do these passages point to the gospel?

How should you respond to these Scriptures? What specific action steps can you take this week to apply them in your life?

Write a prayer in response to your study of God's Word. Adore God for who He is, confess sins He revealed in your own life, ask Him to empower you to walk in obedience, and pray for anyone who comes to mind as you study.

DAY 23

> HE TAKES WHAT THE WORLD SEES AS SMALL, INSIGNIFICANT, AND USELESS AND USES IT FOR HIS GLORY.

The Feeding of the Five Thousand

READ JOHN 6:1-15

As Jesus traveled from region to region, huge crowds followed Him because of His tender care and miraculous healing of the sick. Even when Jesus crossed the Sea of Galilee, the people followed. Not even a body of water could limit them, for they were desperate for the healing touch of Christ.

Though the most important healing Jesus gives us is spiritual, He also cares for our physical needs. He is the faithful Shepherd King promised throughout the Old Testament, who sees the needs of His sheep and delights in meeting them (Jeremiah 23:4-6). While having crowds of people follow Him from day to day certainly fatigued Him, He continued to attend to them. This was not begrudging work for Him. It was what He loved to do and still loves to do! Jesus's healing miracles restored people to the life they were meant to live—physically whole, provided for, and enjoying His presence. They give us a glimpse of our eternal future with Him.

In Luke's account of this miracle, he mentions that Jesus and His disciples withdrew privately to be alone once they crossed the Sea of Galilee (Luke 9:10). The people followed Him here, and as Jesus saw the crowds of people, He did not turn them away. Instead, He paused and asked His disciple, Philip, where they would buy bread for the people to eat. Jesus knew exactly how He was going to provide food for these crowds, but He tested Philip and His disciples to see how they would respond. Philip, overwhelmed by the crowds and calculating the amount of money it would take to feed them all, told Jesus that two hundred denarii would not even be enough to fulfill Jesus's request. Philip was purposefully dramatic in saying this. Two hundred denarii were more than six months' wages, and even that large sum of money could not buy all the bread they would need.

But Jesus was testing Philip. His disciples had seen Him perform great miracles before, and this time would be no different. Jesus would meet the physical needs of the hungry, desperate crowds, and He foreshadowed what He had come to earth to accomplish.

The gospel writer, John, emphasizes that at the time of this miracle, it was nearing Passover, one of the most important feasts for the Jewish people. Passover was a time for Israel to remember how God delivered them from Egypt. When the Lord sent the final plague that would kill all of the firstborn of Egypt as punishment for not letting His people go, He instructed the Israelites to put the blood of lambs on their doorposts so their firstborn children would be spared (Exodus 12). They were "passed over" as a near-perfect lamb served as a sacrifice to save them.

Andrew brought a small boy to Jesus, and this boy had two fish and five loaves of barley bread. He offered his food for Jesus to have. However, Andrew quipped that the quaint meal was not enough to feed everyone. This young boy gave all he had to Jesus, and Jesus would provide abundantly with his offering. He takes what the world sees as small, insignificant, and useless and uses it for His glory. Jesus instructed the disciples to tell the people to sit down. He gave thanks for the food the Lord provided, and then He began to distribute it among the people. He multiplied the two fish and the five loaves, and He and the disciples passed it out to all of the people until they were satisfied. There were even multiple baskets of leftovers after everyone finished.

When the crowds realized the miraculous work Jesus had accomplished, they recognized that He was a great prophet. They were right. Jesus is the true and better prophet who not only speaks God's Word but is the Word made flesh, and He would deliver so much more than one meal of bread and fish. He is the Word of God in flesh, and He would offer them eternal life.

The people were excited. Jesus was the promised Messiah, and they wanted to make Him king. They were even willing to set Him up as king against His will, but Jesus would not have this, and He withdrew. This miracle intended to point them toward greater things than establishing an earthly kingdom. Jesus was trying to point them toward a heavenly kingdom.

With Passover in mind, Jesus beckoned the people to see Him as doing the same thing the Lord had done for their ancestors in the wilderness after they left Egypt. These people were in a desolate place just like the wilderness, and the Lord nourished them just as He did their ancestors. They did not yet know that Jesus would also become the perfect Passover Lamb who would offer Himself as a sacrifice so that the Lord passed over the sins of His people. As He broke the bread and gave it to the five thousand, He foreshadowed how He would give His own body for the sins of the world. Jesus would soon teach His disciples to break bread to remember His body that He would give for them. And this astounding miracle points toward this truth.

Furthermore, this great feast in a desolate place full of hungry people foreshadowed another feast that Jesus will host with all the people from every generation who choose to follow Him as their Lord and Savior—the wedding feast of the Lamb and His bride (Revelation 19:6-9). We will one day sit at the Lord's table and feast with our bridegroom, and just like the five thousand who were fully satisfied and fed, we also will be satisfied in Christ. But the difference between them and us is that when we arrive at this feast, we will no longer feel hunger or need because Jesus will have restored all things forever.

day twenty-three questions

What did you learn about the character of our Savior toward those in need from this passage? How does knowing this about His character encourage you?

Read Luke 22:7-20. How was the Lord's Supper foreshadowed in this miracle?

Take a moment to write a prayer of praise for the coming feast you will someday attend with Him in eternity.

DAY 24

> LIKE THE MANNA WHICH CAME FROM HEAVEN, JESUS HAD COME DOWN FROM HEAVEN TO GIVE LIFE TO HIS PEOPLE.

Bread of Life

READ JOHN 6:22-71

The context surrounding John 6 has its roots in Passover, a Jewish holiday, and the wilderness period. Passover commemorated when the Israelites escaped slavery in Egypt and was celebrated by eating unleavened bread or bread without yeast. This bread was a sign of their trust in God, as they left Egypt quickly and did not have the time to take risen bread. In Exodus 16, the Israelites grew weary on the way to the land God promised them and complained about the wilderness conditions. They lost sight of God and His promises and were distracted by their physical desires. Hearing their cries, God provided manna, a sweet, wafer-like substance that the Israelites could use for breadmaking. Everyone who gathered the manna each morning had enough for that day. The manna was a sign of God's grace and their need to depend on Him every day to provide.

These events were in the backdrop of John 6, as the time of Passover was near. Jesus had performed healing miracles during His ministry, and many followed Him. The crowd grew to 5,000, and Jesus multiplied the fish and loaves of bread to feed them, as we saw in yesterday's passage. This scene was different from the exodus and the harsh wilderness conditions for the Israelites. The unleavened bread of Passover was taken in flight and eaten in haste. Additionally, in the desert, there was a lack of water and vegetation. But, in the presence of the Son of God, there was true rest, comfort, and peace as He worked on their behalf. Jesus distributed the loaves and the fish to all the people who reclined leisurely in the grass. Remember, the amount of manna was only enough to collect for one day. But, in John 6, Jesus multiplied the loaves and fish so that there was plenty leftover. Jesus demonstrated both divine provision and abundance.

The next day, the crowd went to look for Jesus. But, they were searching to satisfy their physical desires again. Jesus pointed them to food that does not perish. Jesus told them only the Son of Man provides this type of food which does not perish but gives eternal life (John 6:27). Jesus emphasized belief in Him to receive this gift. The people then asked for a sign and compared Jesus to Moses, who gave their ancestors manna in the wilderness. They had forgotten the miraculous feeding the day before. Jesus declared that He was the true "bread of life" (John 6:35). Like the manna which came from heaven, Jesus had come down from heaven to give life to His people. As the Son of God, He was completing the will of God the Father and fulfilling what the story of Moses and the wilderness period signified. Jesus Himself would give life to those who were perishing. Manna was a sign of the true bread to come in Christ, but it was insufficient to provide the Israelites spiritual nourishment. Though it kept them alive in the wilderness, the manna would not ultimately save them from sin and death. Instead, they needed to partake of Jesus, the true bread of life. The people needed to feed on His flesh and drink His blood (John 6:54). Jesus used this figurative language to show deep intimacy. When we consume food, in a way it becomes one with us. In John 6:56, Jesus stated, "The one who eats my flesh and drinks my blood remains in me, and I in him." This oneness with Christ is necessary to receive eternal satisfaction in the presence of God. But, hardened by their sin, the people did not understand. The crowd, and even some disciples, were offended by this message and left Jesus. However, through the revelation of the Holy Spirit, the disciples remaining deepened their faith in the One with words of life.

Like the Israelites and the crowd in John 6, we seek God for physical satisfaction rather than spiritual satisfaction. We follow Jesus for certain earthly desires and hope He will cater to our idols. At times, we may come to God with demands of better finances, marriage, health, or success. God does desire to see us redeemed and flourishing in all areas of life, but ultimately, those things are temporary and are supposed to point to the greater, spiritual flourishing we have in Christ. The gift of eternal life has been given to us who believe in Jesus. We navigate this life with the presence of God living inside us. His constant presence nourishes our souls. His grace is like the bread we need for daily sustenance. With this kind of bread, there is no lack. It is rich and abundant. We must depend on the saving work of Jesus every day so that we can resist sin and be strengthened to fight against the pulls of our flesh. Let us deepen our trust in Jesus Christ so that we may always perceive God's truth beyond our temporary desires.

> "THE MANNA WAS A SIGN OF GOD'S GRACE AND THEIR NEED TO DEPEND ON HIM EVERY DAY TO PROVIDE.

day twenty-four questions

The people heard Jesus's message, but they did not perceive the spiritual meaning. What does John 6:44 reveal about this?

What are some areas in your life where you may tend to prioritize physical blessing over spiritual truth?

Write out a prayer asking for help in gaining an eternal perspective and deepening your dependence on Jesus.

DAY 25

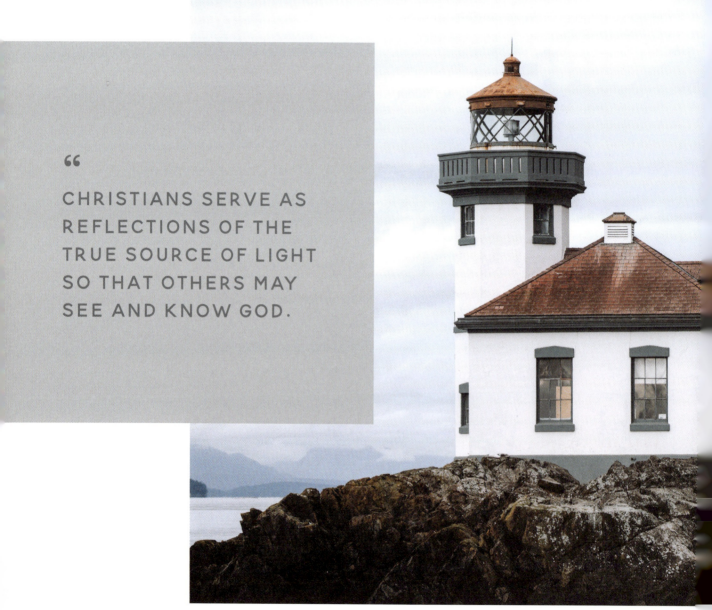

> CHRISTIANS SERVE AS REFLECTIONS OF THE TRUE SOURCE OF LIGHT SO THAT OTHERS MAY SEE AND KNOW GOD.

Light of the World

READ JOHN 8:12, PSALM 43:3, MATTHEW 5:14-16

In the first chapter of Genesis, God speaks, "Let there be light," and light is brought forth sheerly by His voice. This light exposed the work that God was about to put on display in the world. Then God made the sun, moon, and stars to be physical lights. Had there never been a distinguished physical light, how would we see tangible and detailed evidence of our Creator's handiwork in creation? Imagine living and moving and having our being with no physical light. This physical light is good and serves us in more ways than we can possibly fathom. But physical light is a mere shadow of a more necessary light. The created intention of physical light, however, is to point us to a greater, spiritual light—a light so necessary that the Son of God came to declare and impart it to men. John 8:12 reads, "Jesus spoke to them again: 'I am the light of the world. Anyone who follows me will never walk in the darkness but will have the light of life.'" This scriptural analogy speaks of God's illuminated truth—the lighting of His Word as revealed through life in Christ.

The book of John begins with affirming Jesus's Trinitarian presence in the very beginning. He was fully involved in creating the world with God, and all things were made through Him. John recounts, "In Him was life, and that life was the light of men. That light shines in the darkness, and yet the darkness did not overcome it" (John 1:4-5). This reference of Jesus being the spiritual light is continuous throughout Scripture. It brings to the forefront Christ's illuminating sacrifice of love intended to pierce dark hearts and bring them to the light. Without Him, we would never know the truth, and we would never see the way to eternal life.

The light revealed through the life of Jesus Christ dives deep into the sinful, darkened hearts of men and illuminates a way out of this darkness. This is the hope of the gospel. As we understand who Jesus is and what

He has done, we are called out of the darkness and called into His salvific light. Through salvation, we see the world in the way God intends for us to see it. Just as a glowing lantern pierces through the wandering darkness, so the light of truth pierces through the depths of spiritual darkness. Sin has made our hearts dark to the truth of God. We want our own way, and we will wander forever searching for it. The only way we escape the darkness of the sin we have entangled ourselves in is through the revelation of the knowledge of God displayed in our hearts. That revelation comes only through salvation in Jesus Christ. This hope is affirmed in 2 Corinthians 4:6, "For God who said, 'Let light shine out of darkness,' has shown in our hearts to give the light of the knowledge of God's glory in the face of Christ."

Through repentant hearts changed by the truth of the gospel, we are enabled to see the work of Christ in our lives and the world. We can walk forward with visible hope. This spiritual light clears a path for us and exposes what is hidden in the dark. If left unexposed, it only grows and entangles us. But with the Word of God at work in our hearts and the help of the Holy Spirit shaping us, hidden realities of sin that we may be tempted to ignore are continually brought to the light. God equips us to walk in the light and fight the darkness. And He promises that if we remain in the light, the darkness will never overcome us. We are assured and secure in our salvation.

Jesus is the Light of the World. If we remain in Christ, we will never find ourselves wandering without purpose again. We, too, are called to be witnesses of the light. In Matthew 5:14-16, Christians are depicted as the light of the world. Christians serve as reflections of the true source of light so that others may see and know God.

Looking back to the light brought forth in the opening lines of Genesis 1, we can identify that its source was not the sun. It existed apart from any physical light because the sun, moon, and stars were not created until Genesis 1:14-19. Though we have a physical light now to make things visible to us in this life, they will burn out and die in time. But we see a glimpse into this beginning light that lit up the world and will shine forever in eternity. Revelation 21:23 reveals that in the new heavens and new earth, we will not need a physical light, but the glory of God gives its light, and the Lamb is its lamp. Jesus is the Light of the World. From the beginning of creation and on into eternity, He shines bright the hope of eternity with God that awaits all who put their faith and hope in Him.

> "AS WE UNDERSTAND WHO JESUS IS AND WHAT HE HAS DONE, WE ARE CALLED OUT OF THE DARKNESS AND CALLED INTO HIS SALVIFIC LIGHT.

day twenty-five questions

In your own words, write what is meant by the words, "Jesus is the light of the world."

Light exposes what is in the dark. In what ways have you personally experienced the exposure of your sin through life in Jesus Christ?

What hope do you find in Jesus Christ as our eternal light, and what comfort do you find in hearing that with Him we will never live in darkness again?

In what ways can you serve as a beacon of light to those whose hearts are darkened to the truth of the gospel?

DAY 26

> HE WILL ALWAYS KEEP US SAFE AND SECURE IN HIS HAND, AND NOTHING CAN SEPARATE US FROM HIM.

The Good Shepherd

READ JOHN 10:1-21

One of the most frequently used pieces of imagery throughout the Bible is the imagery of shepherds and sheep. Culturally, shepherds and sheep were well known to the Jewish people, so it is no wonder that Jesus uses them as examples in His teaching. Not only this, but in today's passage, Jesus uses these examples to communicate two major "I am" statements. These statements explain who He is and how to identify those who belong to Him.

In context, these words from Jesus in chapter 10 occur after the healing of the blind man. Chapter 9 of John ended with Jesus confronting the Pharisees over their guilt, so chapter 10 is a natural continuation of that conversation. In this passage, the word picture Jesus gives is a large sheep pen with several groups of sheep inside. An undershepherd or watchman guards the sheep pen. Those authorized to enter would be recognized by the watchman, allowing them to enter through the gate. But those who were not authorized, but wanted to get in, would break in by their own means.

Jesus calls out those who avoid the gate by referring to them as thieves and robbers. They are strangers to the sheep pen, unauthorized to enter in through the gate, so they climb in instead. But unlike them, the shepherd, having authority, goes through the door. Because he is no stranger to the sheep pen, the sheep in his care recognize his voice and follow him as he brings them out. The sheep will not follow the voice of strangers because they are accustomed to the voice of their master alone. Jesus knows His sheep by name and calls them to Him, showing their intimate relationship with Him. Knowing Jesus is like knowing a friend or a family member. If they call our names, we automatically recognize their voices and know we can trust them. But if strangers call out to us, we do not immediately trust them because we do not know them. By drawing this first comparison, Jesus made a distinction between Himself and the Pharisees. The Pharisees were the thieves and robbers who ridiculed the sheep rather than take care of them. Jesus is the Shepherd who has authority from His Father to care for those who belong to Him.

The Pharisees did not understand this figure of speech Jesus was using to teach them, so Jesus shifted to another analogy. Now, Jesus compared Himself to the door of the sheep pen and made His first "I am" statement of the passage: "I am the gate for the sheep" (John 10:7). In doing so, Jesus established Himself as the only way a sheep can enter into the flock. Any who came before Him professing a way to enter are thieves or false teachers who preach false salvation. As the door, Jesus designates Himself as the one true way for salvation, and those who enter in receive everlasting life. Whereas the thief comes to bring death by hurt and manipulation, Jesus has come to bring abundant life.

Jesus then moved to His second "I am" statement: "I am the good shepherd" (John 10:11). By this statement, Jesus was speaking to how He brings about abundant life for His sheep. He declared Himself as the way to salvation, and here He declared how He brings about such salvation. Jesus is the Good Shepherd because He loves His sheep so much that He is willing to die for them. He is not like a hired hand who is reckless with the sheep in his care, who flees in the face of danger and causes his sheep to be devoured by wolves. Instead, Jesus lays His life down to bring salvation for His sheep. His sheep are not strangers to Him. In owning them, they have an intimate relationship with Him. Just like Jesus has an intimate relationship with the Father, so He has an intimate relationship with His sheep, who are believers. Jesus also pointed out that there are more who belong to the flock. As the Good Shepherd, He must bring those outside the flock in as well. Here, Jesus is talking about the Gentiles or non-Jewish people. The Jews that God has sovereignly called to salvation are not the only ones who will belong to the kingdom of God. God has also called Gentiles to saving faith—those who will join the other people as one flock, one body of Christ.

By laying down His life and taking it up again, Jesus pointed to His death and resurrection. He would one day lay His life down by dying on a cross and would take it back up again by His resurrection. His death and resurrection would provide the way for those God has called to come to salvation, entering into an everlasting life of abundance and intimacy with their Good Shepherd.

This passage teaches two major lessons. First, it speaks to God's sovereignty. God, in His merciful sovereignty, has called us to salvation. His plan for salvation will not be thwarted, whether it be by false teachers or pious religious leaders. By sending His Son, God has saved His chosen people. In His sovereignty, He has also included those whom the Pharisees looked down upon in their pride. He has created a family of both Jew and Gentile where they can all be one, reflecting the words of Paul in Galatians 3:28, "There is no Jew or Greek, slave or free, male and female; since you are all one in Christ Jesus." Second, the passage speaks to God's way of salvation. Jesus is the door to salvation; He is the one true way of knowing Him, to have an intimate relationship with Him. No other "doors" will lead to this salvation but the salvation that comes from believing in Jesus.

As our Good Shepherd, Jesus brings comfort to us as believers. As His sheep, we have an intimate relationship with Him who knows us by name. He will always keep us safe and secure in His hand, and nothing can separate us from Him. In John 10:28, Jesus says, "I give them eternal life, and they will never perish. No one will snatch them out of my hand." When we doubt our salvation or fear that God has released His grip on us, this passage helps us rest with confidence in Him. And as we continue through our lives, we can rest assured that our Shepherd leads us to eternity. Being a part of God's flock means we also get to share in it with others. He is not just leading you into eternity but every other sheep that is called to be a part of this flock. This should give us great love for the other members of the flock. Jesus has one flock, one body of Christ that by His great love we share in together. May we all remain obedient to our Good Shepherd by listening to His voice as He guides us into eternity.

day twenty-six questions

Read Ezekiel 34. How does Jesus fulfill this passage?

Read Psalm 23. How does this passage bring you comfort?
What does it say about our Good Shepherd?

Even in an intimate relationship with God, we can easily be caught up by other voices.
What is keeping you from following the voice of Jesus in your daily life?

DAY 27

> WE CAN REST, KNOWING THAT GOD'S LOVE FOR US IS SECURE.

Jesus Reveals Himself

READ MATTHEW 16:13-20

In Matthew 16:13, Jesus asked His followers, "Who do people say that the Son of Man is?" Several of the disciples chipped in, "Some say John the Baptist; others, Elijah; still others, Jeremiah or one of the prophets." Jesus then pressed in further, asking, "who do you say that I am?" This time, only one person responded. Peter proclaimed, "You are the Messiah, the Son of the living God."

Thinking about it, Peter could have responded to this question in many truthful ways: Jesus, You are the carpenter from Nazareth; You are my friend; You are a great leader who has caused a revival in the hearts of Your people; You are a great teacher; You are the healer; You are mysterious; You are a prophet who speaks with all authority. But He responded with ultimate boldness saying, "You are the Son of God, the Messiah." Jesus commended Peter for his answer, reminding him that this belief comes only from God.

Because of God's grace, Peter recognized the power of Jesus's teachings—that Jesus claimed to be God and asserted authority and power over all creation. Peter also recognized the significance of these claims. Peter left his career, his family, his reputation, and his comfort to follow this one true God.

Peter could have assumed he was a disciple of Jesus because he was around Jesus a lot. He saw Jesus do miracles, traveled and ate with Him, and sat under His teaching. But to affirm the deity of Christ was an essential step in Peter's story. Similarly, when we come to Jesus, it is not enough to live off of the faith of others. If we were born into a Christian family, we could easily assume that we are saved because we were raised in the church. Conversely, if we are the only person in our family who goes to church, it is easy to believe that we are a Christian because we are different from our family. However, the act of going to church does not make you a Christian. To be cleansed of our sins and made right with God, we each must confess our sins and turn to the risen Christ.

So who do you, dear reader, say that He is? For if Jesus is Lord, this truly changes everything. He promises eternal life for those who trust in Him. He saves us from death, forgives us, and brings us into new life. He makes us His friends, though we were once His enemies. Because of Jesus's perfect life, death, and resurrection, we can joyfully submit to a loving Savior, to the One who knows us and protects us. We no longer need to strive to be accepted or seek out redemption for ourselves. We can rest, knowing that God's love for us is secure. No longer do we groan under the burdensome Law, condemned by our failures. Instead, Jesus paid the penalty of our debt by dying on the cross for us. Such an amazing truth changes everything about the way we live today. It changes the way we spend our money, use our time, and treat others. It changes our allegiances and our desires. No longer do we live trying to have our best life now. Our best life is hidden with Christ in heaven, and one day we will see Him face-to-face.

And still, sometimes, following Jesus requires great sacrifice today. To follow Christ means professing faith in a potentially hostile world. Many who met Jesus on Earth would not believe Him to be Lord, and Peter would eventually be killed for the belief he so boldly asserted. When we confess Jesus as Lord, the world and the flesh may turn against us. We may receive hatred from our friends or family. We may be disowned or cast out of our towns. But our Savior is worth all of these sacrifices, and we confess Him as Lord, regardless of the cost. We surrender our lives to Him, risking rejection and persecution for the sake of His name, for we know that for those who believe, even death does not have the final word. Our hope is in a risen Christ, who will one day return to make all things right. We will have a joy that surpasses all the pleasures of this world and will be reunited with Him. On this day, there will be no more suffering or trials or pain. He will finally return to make all things new.

Jesus is the gentle Shepherd who came to pave the way for salvation for His people. He is the righteous judge and the fulfillment of the Law. He is the Holy One, immaculate in all His ways. He is the King who came to redeem His people. He is our friend, who knows our pains and sorrows. He is the Lord.

> **BECAUSE OF JESUS'S PERFECT LIFE, DEATH, AND RESURRECTION, WE CAN JOYFULLY SUBMIT TO A LOVING SAVIOR, TO THE ONE WHO KNOWS US AND PROTECTS US.**

day twenty-seven questions

Have you submitted to Jesus in every area of your life? Spend time reflecting on any areas of hidden sin or fears of publicly identifying with Christ.

Read Matthew 10:32-33. What are some of the consequences of fearing men more than God?

Read Romans 1:16. Pray for boldness and that you would not be ashamed of the power of the gospel. Pray that the Lord would open the eyes of your friends and family members who are not yet saved.

DAY 28

> AS CHRIST HAS LOVED US, SO LET US LOVE ONE ANOTHER.

The Good Samaritan

READ LUKE 10:25-37

In today's story, an expert of the Law came to Jesus. This lawyer was a man of conviction and integrity, literally upholding the Law as his profession. At the time, such a man would have been highly esteemed in the community, wealthy and well-educated. As the lawyer stood before Jesus, he asked, "Teacher, what must I do to inherit eternal life?" At first glance, it seems like the man was asking Jesus a great question. It is the question we would want all our church members, children, and family to ask. But in Luke 10:25, Scripture reveals that the man did not come humbly, desiring help from Jesus. He came trying to trap Him.

Knowing the man's motives, Jesus asked the man what the Law said. The man responded by reciting Deuteronomy 6:5 and Leviticus 19:18—that we are to love the Lord our God with all our hearts, souls, mind, and strength, and we are to love our neighbor as ourselves. Jesus affirmed the man's words saying, "Do this and you will live." How great is this command—love the Lord with all your heart, soul, mind, and strength. Have no idols before Him. Obey Him no matter what. Put Him first in your life. This task in itself is beyond comprehension, impossible to grasp. Furthermore, to love our neighbors as ourselves is seemingly unattainable. We are very self-centered people. Not many of us feed, clothe, and buy treats for others as we do for ourselves. We do not easily show grace to others or forgive them when they sin. Yet, we are very quick to pamper and show grace to ourselves.

Turning our focus back to the rich man, Jesus's answer did not satisfy the man, who wanted to justify himself further. He wanted to prove that he was good enough and asked the follow-up question, "And who is my neighbor?" Jesus responded by telling the story of a man who took the dangerous journey down from Jerusalem to Jericho. The trip was treacherous. It was rough and rocky, with many spots for hiding bandits and threatening encounters on the path. It was so dangerous that it even earned the nickname the "path of blood." As the man was traveling down this road from Jerusalem to Jericho, robbers attacked him, beat him, and stole everything he had. They left him, bloodied and bruised, close to death.

Around the time they left him for dead, a priest was also traveling down the road. When he saw the man beaten and bloody, he passed by on the other side of the road. Perhaps the priest thought the bandits were nearby, and he was afraid that he would be beaten, too. Were robbers lying in wait for Him, just out of sight behind the rocks? Was this a trap? The journey down the "path of blood" was so dangerous that it would have been too dangerous to stop.

Another possibility for him not stopping was that the priest came from Jerusalem, where he would have just purified himself for his religious duties. If he were to touch any dead object, he would become ceremonially dirty. He would need to take another trip to the temple, adding at least seven days for purification to his journey. That would have been inconvenient to both himself and those he was trying to serve. Later, a Levite passed by the same place. The Levite was also a religious man, who valued the Law, but he too saw the bloodied man and passed by on the other side. Not desiring to dirty himself, he went on his way, either too busy or too fearful to stop along such a dangerous route.

Finally, a Samaritan came down the path. Samaritans were half-Jewish, half-Gentile, tracing their lineage back to the Assyrian invasion of Israel; they were not friends with the Jews. They were considered unclean, and to even share bread with a Samaritan was abhorrent.

Yet, despite their differences, the Samaritan went to the man, kneeled, and took care of his bloody wounds. He took the olive oil and wine he had prepared for his journey and poured them on the man. He used his money and his resources to bandage him. Then, the Samaritan put the man on his animal, choosing to walk down the bumpy path himself. He brought the man to an inn and promised to pay all the expenses for his care. Jesus concluded his story with a question, "Which of these three do you think proved to be a neighbor to the man who fell into the hands of the robbers?" The man answered, "The one who showed mercy to him."

Often when we hear this story, we insert ourselves as the "good guy," the Good Samaritan who selflessly serves others with joy and at great personal cost. But Jesus was suggesting the opposite. If we were to insert ourselves into this story, we would not be the Good Samaritan but the helpless, bloodied man, unable to save ourselves. Jesus is the Good Samaritan who had compassion on us, coming to save us at great sacrifice to Himself. Christ rescued us when we were unworthy, completely in sin due to our own decisions. He bought our redemption. More than the Good Samaritan, though, Jesus took our place, giving Himself for us so that we could be made clean.

In response to Christ's great love for us, we are called to love others, even those who are different from us. We are even called to love our enemies, whether they are on opposite sides of the world or in opposing political parties. In light of this story, we must also consider: If we are obeying the Ten Commandments but not loving those around us, has the gospel's message really changed us? How are we responding to the hurting people around us? Do we withdraw, not wanting to dirty our lives? Do we watch them from a distance but decide that we are quite satisfied with our safe, comfortable lives? Are we too busy or too clean to help someone else? Or do we follow the example of Jesus, who entered into the pain and suffering at great cost to Himself? As Christ has loved us, so let us love one another.

day twenty-eight questions

In what ways is Jesus like the Good Samaritan? In what ways are they different?

Read Deuteronomy 6:5 and Micah 6:8. How does God's love for you change the way that you treat others?

From this story, we learn that we can follow all the rules and still be far from God. What role can legalism play in the Christian faith?

Reflection

REVIEW ALL PASSAGES FROM THE LAST 6 DAYS

Summarize the main points from this week's Scripture readings.

What did you observe from this week's passages about the life of Jesus and His character?

What do this week's passages reveal about the condition of mankind and yourself?

How do these passages point to the gospel?

How should you respond to these Scriptures? What specific action steps can you take this week to apply them in your life?

Write a prayer in response to your study of God's Word. Adore God for who He is, confess sins He revealed in your own life, ask Him to empower you to walk in obedience, and pray for anyone who comes to mind as you study.

DAY 29

> WE WILL FOREVER MARVEL AT THE BEAUTY OF JESUS, THANKFUL AND PRAISING HIM FOR HIS SAVING WORK.

The Transfiguration

READ MATTHEW 17:1-8, MARK 9:2-8, LUKE 9:26-36

Matthew, Mark, and Luke all noted the transfiguration of Jesus in their gospel accounts. In their Jewish context, the disciples wrote about this event with an understanding of theophanies recorded in the Old Testament. A theophany was a visible manifestation of the Lord's presence and power. God used theophanies for His redemptive purposes—to ultimately save His people from sin and death through the coming Savior. A mountain was a significant location for theophanies. There, God met with those He appointed for divine leadership. An example of a theophany in the Old Testament is Exodus 34. God descended on Mount Sinai in a thick cloud and spoke with Moses. Then, God showed Moses His "back," or a partial view of His glory, as He pronounced His righteous, faithful, and loving character. Scripture tells us that when Moses came down from this encounter, his face was "transfigured" into something beautiful and radiant.

Theophanies in the Old Testament are in the background of today's passages. About a week before the transfiguration, Jesus predicted His death and resurrection (Luke 9:21-22). Peter, one of the disciples hearing this prediction, rebuked Jesus. Peter believed Jesus was a political Savior and could not be defeated by death. Jesus pointed out that Satan was now at work and that Peter did not have a spiritual perspective (Mark 8:32-33). Christ did not come to be a great political leader but to save His people from sin and judgment through His death on the cross. Jesus emphasized the suffering that awaited Him and anyone who followed Him. But, the one who sacrificed temporary pleasures for the gospel would receive eternal life (Matthew 16:25). In light of this conversation, Jesus took Peter and two other disciples, James and John, to a mountain to pray. The disciples fell asleep, but Jesus continued to pray into the night. While He was praying, His face was transfigured, and the disciples woke up to this awesome sight. Like the light of the sun, His face was radiant and awe-inspiring. His clothes were bright white and dazzling. Moses's transfiguration pointed to Jesus's transfiguration in the New Testament. However, scholars point out that the fading light on Moses was limited to his face. Jesus's light radiated from his entire appearance, proving His divine identity.

Then, Moses and Elijah appeared with Jesus and talked to Him about His "departure" (Luke 9:31). Scholars explain that the word translated as "departure" can also mean "death." The presence of Moses, who represented the Old Testament law, and Elijah, who represented the Old Testament prophets, was significant. Their appearance solidified Jesus as the fulfillment of the Law and prophecy. Through His saving work, Jesus would accomplish all of what the Old Testament predicted—that the Anointed One would come from heaven to be a suffering servant for God's people and redeem His broken world. The conversation between Moses, Elijah, and Jesus also seemed to comfort Peter, as he offered to build them a shelter so they could stay on the mountain. Peter saw a glimpse of the glory that would be realized in Jesus's resurrection and ascension and seemed not to want it to end. However, this sight was just a foretaste of the beauty and majesty Peter would witness forever in heaven. After the appearance of Moses and Elijah, a thick cloud enveloped them. The disciples were fearful, as such a cloud represented God's holy presence. They also might have been fearful because, in Leviticus 16:2, God tells Moses that if Aaron enters the mercy seat, where God sits in the form of a cloud, he will die. However, they did not die. Instead, God the Father spoke from the cloud, confirming Jesus as the beloved Son. The Father commanded the disciples to listen to Jesus, as He was the ultimate theophany, the full presence of God in flesh.

Imagine an amazing sunset. See the radiance of the sun breaking through the clouds. Gaze at the fractured light bringing about red, orange, yellow, and purple colors. Witness the colors dance across the sky. Hearts lift with wonder and awe. Our spirits are overcome with joy. This illustration is a small picture of what the disciples experienced on the mountain with Jesus. We, who are believers, will see His glory after this life. We, who have kept our eye on the eternal treasure of Jesus, will witness the full presence of God in heaven. Our spirits will be overcome with a joyful fear of the Lord as we are enveloped in His love. We will forever marvel at the beauty of Jesus, thankful and praising Him for His saving work. Purified from sin, we will transfigure into images of glory, mirroring our Savior. Let us awaken our hearts to this truth and set our eyes on the wonderful sight of the cross.

> " CHRIST DID NOT COME TO BE A GREAT POLITICAL LEADER BUT TO SAVE HIS PEOPLE FROM SIN AND JUDGMENT THROUGH HIS DEATH ON THE CROSS.

day twenty-nine questions

Identify another theophany in the Bible.

Read 2 Peter 1:16-21. How does Peter compare the revelation of Scripture to witnessing the transfiguration of Jesus?

How does the hope of glorification inform how you view your body? How do you react to knowing that your physical scars, disabilities, and imperfections will transform into a body of glory (Philippians 3:21) at Jesus's second coming?

DAY 30

> WE CANNOT RUN TOO FAR FROM GOD, NOR CAN WE EARN OUR WAY INTO HIS PRESENCE.

Parable of the Prodigal Son

READ LUKE 15:11-32

There is something to be gathered from every parable Jesus ever told. The intended teaching speaks relevantly to all who hear it. When He shared the parable of the prodigal son, it is important to note the audience to which He was speaking. Tax collectors, sinners, Pharisees, and teachers of the Law all held a seat in the room. Starkly different people, and yet Jesus had something to say to all of them.

The parable centers around a family: a father and his older and younger son. The younger son asked his father to distribute the assets of his estate to his two sons. Asking for an inheritance while the father was still living was one of the most dishonorable requests one could make. According to Old Testament law, the father would give a double portion to the firstborn, and the younger son would receive one-third of the property (Deuteronomy 21:17). This type of gift could impede the father's stability to live, and yet he gifted the two sons with their shares. Each took their inheritance but handled it very differently. The older stayed home and worked for his father and did what seemed most honorable. But, the younger son took all that he had been given and traveled to a distant country where he wasted his money on foolish things until he had nothing. As a result, the younger son was forced to take a job feeding pigs, an animal Jewish people regarded as unclean under dietary laws. Can you imagine how humiliated the young son must have felt? He was given everything he needed, yet instead of treasuring it up and stewarding it well, he wasted it all.

When the young son found himself in the most desperate place, he remembered how well he had been cared for by his father, and he longed to return to him. But he likely felt ashamed and embarrassed. How could he return to his father after what he had done? How would he possibly be welcomed back home? But eventually, the young son decided to return home and seek forgiveness. Upon his return home, the father saw him off in the distance and was filled with compassion. He ran to his son and embraced him. His compassionate love led him to move toward his son. It led him to welcome and forgive him instead of cast out and condemn him. It exemplified a loving father willing to lay down his son's transgressions against him and open his gracious arms to receive him. The father called for his servants to adorn his son with a fine robe, ring, and sandals and to slaughter a calf for a feast on his behalf. Not only did the father welcome him back in, but he also wanted to throw a celebration for his son's return! This would have been incredibly unexpected after the son's shameful actions. The younger son was pleading only to be hired for work, but the father invited him back in as his beloved son.

The older son's response to his brother's return was great displeasure for the graces shown. He likely wondered how his father could celebrate such dishonor and foolishness. He had proven himself to be so much more righteous and honorable than his younger brother, and yet he had never received such a feast. When the father learned that the older brother would not celebrate, he went out to him. He urged him and shared what the older son was neglecting to see: "this brother of yours was dead and is alive again; he was lost and is found."

The older brother and the younger brother responded differently to their father's gracious gift. The younger brother squandered the gift offered to him and felt too ashamed to return to his father. Just like the tax collectors and sinners, they were dishonoring God with their lives and often felt they had run too far away to be welcomed by Him. The older brother, however, offered another response. He received his father's gift and continued to work and live in an outwardly honorable way. But he revealed his heart through the return of his younger brother. The older brother felt as if he earned favor with the father and was more deserving of acceptance, just like the Pharisees and the teachers of the law who revelled in self-righteousness and looked down on those they felt were unworthy to be in Jesus's presence.

Both reactions point to a misunderstanding of the gospel of grace. We cannot run too far from God, nor can we earn our way into His presence. God displays the greatest act of grace by offering the free gift of salvation through the sacrifice of His Son, Jesus Christ. Through receiving it, God welcomes us into His family as His beloved children. It is not of our own doing that we are offered a reunion with the Father, but because "God, who is rich in mercy, because of his great love that he had for us, made us alive with Christ even though we were dead in trespasses. [We] are saved by grace!" (Ephesians 2:4-5). His grace is just that: grace. It is a free, unmerited gift offered to us. Ephesians 2:8-9 affirms, "For you are saved by grace through faith, and this is not from yourselves; it is God's gift—not from works, so that no one can boast."

The father in the parable exemplified the kind of selfless and underserved love we experience from God. His gracious love is not a conditional gift but consistent with His nature. It knows no bounds. It far exceeds the depth of our brokenness and the heights of our best efforts. It is unbiased and unrelenting. The hope offered through this parable is not that we will receive His grace if we work hard enough to please God, nor is it that if we run too far away from Him, His grace is lost. Through this parable, the hope offered is that God made a way for us to experience grace as we have never known, and that gift has nothing to do with us but everything to do with Him.

day thirty questions

Which brother's response do you resonate with more? How does the gospel refute both of their responses?

Read Ephesians 2:1-10. In what ways do you misunderstand the gospel of grace? How does this passage speak into those misunderstandings?

Meditate on the grace of God offered to us through salvation in Jesus Christ.

DAY 31

> THROUGH BELIEF IN THE LORD, WE CAN BE DELIVERED FROM SPIRITUAL DEATH AND INTO EVERLASTING LIFE.

Raising of Lazarus

READ JOHN 11:1-44

Jesus was with His disciples when a messenger brought news from Mary and Martha that their brother, Lazarus, was sick. Even though we do not know much about these three from today's story, the close relationship Jesus had with them is evident, as the sisters' message is, "Lord, the one you love is sick." Lazarus's sisters knew Jesus loved their brother and had the power to heal him, so their message is urgent.

Jesus's response to the sisters' message seems puzzling. The sisters feared that Lazarus's illness would lead to his death, however, Jesus said that it would instead lead to God's glory. But Jesus's actions are even more puzzling because He decides to remain where He was. John 11:5 says that Jesus loved Mary and Martha, so when He heard Lazarus was sick, He stayed two days. Jesus's decision to stay connects with the purpose of Lazarus's illness in John 11:4. He will use this delay to reveal His glory in a way we cannot yet see.

After waiting two days, Jesus told the disciples He would go and wake Lazarus from sleep. Misinterpreting His words to mean actual sleep, the disciples thought Jesus was preparing to wake Lazarus from a nap. But Jesus clarified, telling them that Lazarus had died. Not only this, but He also said that it was good He was not yet there to help Lazarus because the following event would help them believe. So even in their confusion, the disciples went with Jesus.

When Martha heard that Jesus had come, she went to meet Him. In a statement of grief, she told Jesus that Lazarus would not have died if He had been there. But she followed up this statement with one of seeming trust and belief, saying that even in this tragedy, she knew God could give Jesus the power to do anything. Martha's statement is likely more of an expression of belief in Jesus as the Son of God than a belief that Jesus could resurrect Lazarus. The Jewish people believed in a future resurrection at the end of time, in which those who belong to God will rise from the dead and be united with Him. Therefore, Martha had no context for a resurrection that would happen in the present. This is why when Jesus told Martha that her brother would rise again, she agreed, probably thinking He was referring to the resurrection to come. But Jesus graciously corrected her thinking by speaking another "I am" statement: "I am the resurrection and the life" (John 11:25). Jesus taught here that it is He alone who can bring resurrected life.

Martha then calls for Mary to come to Jesus. Mary's words to Jesus are the same as Martha's, except there is no expression of belief. Jesus looks upon Mary's grief and those weeping around her and is deeply moved. There are two possible interpretations to describe Jesus's reaction. One is that Jesus was moved with deep compassion, and the other is that Jesus was moved with anger. Regardless, it is because of His love for Mary, Martha, and Lazarus that He is troubled. Like a loving father, rightly angered and grieved over the sin of his son, Jesus has righteous anger and grief over the sin of the world.

However, Jesus's weeping does not last long. He instructs Martha to remove the stone and reminds her of what she has previously claimed. If she trusts in Jesus, she will see His glory. And so she obeys His command, and the stone is rolled away. Before Jesus does anything else, He prays, and those gathered around can hear His words. He thanks God for listening to the prayers of His Son. This public gratitude is for the belief of the people. They had heard with their own ears about Jesus's connection with God, and now they saw with their eyes the authority given to Him. After His prayer, Jesus commanded Lazarus to come out of the tomb. And so he did. Jesus brought him from death to life.

Through this miracle, Jesus declared that He truly was the resurrection and the life. He used the raising of Lazarus as a way to display the glory and power of God. Only God can raise people from the dead, so as He performed this miracle, He affirmed His authority and deity, glorifying God in the process. And this display of power and glory also caused His disciples and others around Him to believe.

Jesus's miracle gave people a foretaste of what was to come. First, it gave a foretaste of what would occur for Him. By raising Lazarus from the dead, Jesus showed He held power over death. Death would not prevail over Him, and soon He would prove this from His death and resurrection. Second, it gave a foretaste of what is to come for believers. Because Jesus has the power to bring people from life to death, He will do the same for those in Christ. Through belief in the Lord, we can be delivered from spiritual death and into everlasting life. There is security in this life for those who believe because nothing can change the salvation given through Christ. Believers may experience physical death, but this earthly death will be met by everlasting life with Christ.

The purpose of Jesus's miracle was to elicit a response of both belief and worship, and may this be the response of our hearts as well. Jesus is the resurrection and the life. This truth should encourage our hearts in the present as we await the future. By the power of Jesus, we have been brought from death to life in Christ. There is no fear in death because we know that there is only life for the believer in Christ. Let us glorify our God who has conquered the grave and raised us to a renewed life in Him.

day thirty-one questions

Read John 12:10-11. What was the outcome of Jesus's miracle? How does this connect to the purpose of raising Lazarus?

Martha shows great faith, even in her mourning, by trusting in who Jesus is and in God's power. How do you react during times of discouragement or grief? How can you trust God instead of questioning what He is doing?

Read 1 Thessalonians 4:13-18. What should our response be as believers to death? What truths does this passage teach us about our future resurrection and those of other brothers and sisters in Christ?

DAY 32

> "WITH AN ETERNAL PERSPECTIVE, WE KNOW THAT JESUS IS THE ONLY ONE WORTH LIVING FOR.

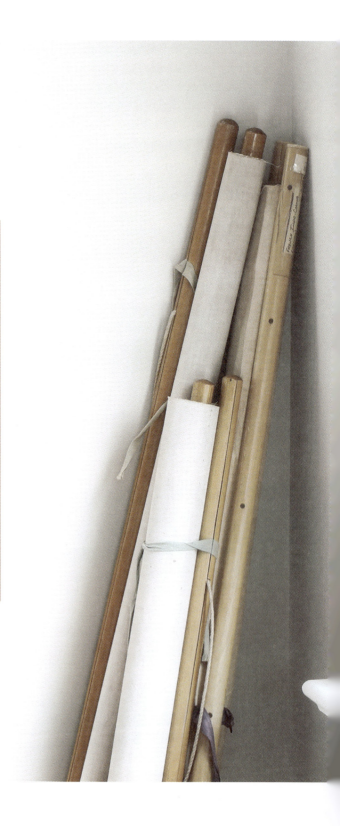

Triumphant Entry

READ MATTHEW 21:1-17, MARK 11:1-11, LUKE 19:29-44, JOHN 12:12-19

As Jesus went up to Jerusalem for Passover in John 12, a large, cheering crowd greeted Him. They gathered enthusiastically and waved palm branches, shouting words of praise. Some spread their cloaks along the road, making a royal carpet of coats. Others took branches and laid them along the road. The crowd waved excitedly, longing for even a glimpse of Jesus. Many had heard of Lazarus rising from the dead and had come to see the One who healed him. Moreover, some heard of His power to multiply food, and others listened to His teaching throughout the region firsthand.

With enthusiasm, the crowd gathered and yelled, "Hosanna to the Son of David! Blessed is He who comes in the name of the Lord! Hosanna in the highest heaven!" (Matthew 21:9). This word "Hosanna" literally means "give salvation now," or in layman's terms, "Yay! Salvation is here!" It affirmed Jesus as the One who could save and was a form of praise. This language echoes Psalm 118:25-26, which says, "Lord, save us! Lord, please grant us success! He who comes in the name of the Lord is blessed. From the house of the Lord we bless you." They were ready to make Jesus the king.

The crowd was hungry and eager for redemption. They desired to submit to Jesus's kind leadership and longed for the freedom He offered. But, unfortunately, the people did not understand Jesus's ultimate purpose. Many of the people were seeking primarily a political healing, not a spiritual one. They did not understand their deeper need for spiritual salvation, nor were they prepared for this Suffering Servant. The crowd did not comprehend the words of Zechariah, which pointed to the true coming King: "Rejoice greatly, Daughter of Zion. Shout in triumph, Daughter Jerusalem! Look, your King is coming to you; he is righteous and victorious, humble and riding on a donkey" (Zechariah

9:9). The strong waving of their palm branches symbolized their desire for liberation from the Romans, not submission to the Prince of Peace.

Although Jesus had prophesied about His life, death, and resurrection, the people still did not understand. They expected Him to take the city by force, enacting immediate social and political change. But Jesus did not come to dispel the powerful Romans or take the city of Jerusalem by political strength. Instead, He came to bear the sins of the people on His broken body. He did not come on a war horse or with grand displays of power. Instead, He came meek and lowly, riding a donkey. He came in weakness, meekness, and humility.

The excitement of the crowd stirred the whole city, and the mob wondered, "Who is this?" The Pharisees and Sadducees particularly were unhappy with His growing popularity, as they felt threatened by His power. And soon, the very crowd who shouted such grandiose words of prayer would turn on Him as well. When Jesus was not exalted as a political revolutionary but instead condemned to a criminal's death, the people quickly deserted Him, calling for His death.

On this side of history, we know the full story. We know that Jesus is the way to eternal life. By believing in His life, death, and resurrection, God will forgive our sins and restore us to Himself. We also know that while a life with Christ offers eternal salvation and grace, it is not without trials. Jesus does not offer us a pain-free life full of material prosperity or a promise that we will live under a perfectly peaceful government. He does not offer us a sickness-free, poverty-free life this side of heaven. He does not always do what we expect. Although Jesus could have started a revolution, freeing the people from a harsh government, He knew their deeper need for salvation from eternal damnation. Through Jesus's perfect sacrifice, He provided a way for them to be saved through faith in Him.

And still, we can often be like the crowd of John 12. Just like the crowd, our affections for Christ can often be short-lived when we are under trial. Though we know that Christ has the power to save, we still want Him to fit the mold we have created and fulfill our desires for a healthy, wealthy life. But in reality, to follow Christ, the suffering servant, means that we will suffer in this life, so we must count the cost. When we face pressure from family or friends for going to church or are mocked for being "too pure," will Christ be enough for us? When we do not get the promotion at work because we are unwilling to manipulate the numbers, is the joy of the Lord still enough for our souls? Or, when we take a stand for the truths of Scripture as it relates to how we view money, recreation, sexuality, or family, and face persecution, will Christ be enough for us? Many today will fall away from Christ when He does not answer their prayers in the way they desire. But if the cancer does not disappear or the debt does not miraculously get paid, will you still serve Him?

With an eternal perspective, we know that Jesus is the only One worth living for. His kingdom lasts forever, and these temporary struggles will cease. His love is sufficient, and His grace is enough. He is the Promised One, and salvation is through Him alone.

day thirty-two questions

Why did the people worship Jesus passionately and then desert Him?

How have you struggled in your faith amid trials?

Read James 1:12. What does the Bible say about endurance and perseverance through trials?

DAY 33

> BY COMING AS GOD IN THE FLESH, JESUS WAS THE ACCESS POINT FOR GOD AND MAN.

Jesus enters the Temple

READ MATTHEW 21:12-13, MARK 11:15-19, LUKE 19:45

As Jesus walked into the temple, He noticed something was not right. Crowds of people were not gathered to pray but to purchase. He saw greedy merchants and buyers taking advantage of God's place of prayer, and He threw them out, overturning their tables.

It is important to understand that this story does not take place in the actual temple building but in the Court of the Gentiles, the outer court of the temple. By law, Jewish people were the only ones who could enter the temple's inner court, and any Gentile who attempted to do so was punished. A market was set up around the court where people could purchase animals for sacrifices. This was especially helpful for those who had traveled far, as they would not have animals to sacrifice. There were also money-changer tables at which people with different coinage could exchange their money for the correct coins to make purchases. While this selling and exchanging was not inherently wrong, it had become corrupt. Not only this, but this market did not need to be set up in such a sacred place.

Jesus drives out every greedy person and turns over every table used for this corrupt business. He follows up His actions by quoting two passages of Scripture together: "It is written, 'My house shall be called a house of prayer,' but you make it a den of robbers." The first part of this quotation is taken from Isaiah 56:7, which is a vision of God's deliverance for His people where His restoration brings about a place of worship for His people. The second part is taken from Jeremiah 7:11, which is a vision of destruction in which God punishes His people for making His temple into a place of corruption. Using these two verses, Jesus exposes the people for their lack of reverence for God's temple. Their sinful choice caused two kinds of ramifications: distraction and desecration.

Setting up their markets in the Court of the Gentiles meant that the Gentiles who gathered for prayer did not have a reverent place to pray. Picture

Gentiles coming to the outer court to pray, and amongst the busy crowd, imagine them trying to find space to kneel down. Kneeling, they hear the buzz of people, animal sounds, and the yelling of market dealers. All of us know how hard it is to remain focused in prayer, but how difficult it must have been in this particular setting. The Jewish people in the inner court likely heard echoes of these sounds as well. The people's worship would have probably been distracted by such a spectacle. But such actions were also desecrating the temple. God's temple was a sacred space of worship. It was a place of reverence and honor to the Lord. But these people made it a place for their selfish gain, fulfilling the idolatry of their hearts rather than worshiping the Lord.

By driving these people away and turning over their tables, Jesus executed righteous anger for people's sins, for it pained Him greatly to see such sin in a place of worship. As God's Son, Jesus had authority over the temple—He had complete control over it. The people's response shows an awareness of this authority, as they are quickly driven away without dispute.

As Jesus took action, He both exposed the people's sin and brought restoration back to the temple. He also called their attention to what matters most: purity of worship. Access to God in prayer is important and to be respected. The sinful acts of the traders and buyers posed a distraction and disruption of necessary prayer to God. God calls us to take the purity of worship seriously, and Jesus's actions point to this. But Jesus's actions also point to something greater. Jesus's reference to both Isaiah 56:7 and Jeremiah 7:11 was a vision of both destruction and deliverance. Jesus's actions in the temple physically accomplished these two things, but they were ultimately a visual demonstration of what He was going to do for all of humanity. By coming as God in the flesh, Jesus was the access point for God and man. Through a violent death, Jesus would deliver people from their sins. He would remove the barrier that stood between God and man and restore a worshipful relationship with God. No longer would man be limited in his access to God. No more would man have to come to a physical temple to worship Him. Those who came to faith in Christ would have access to God forever. In doing so, Jesus would bring about deliverance to the Gentiles. Clearing out the space of the court of Gentiles was a picture of Jesus making a way for Gentiles to have access to God as well. By His death and resurrection, both Jew and Gentile could experience a connection with God in an entirely new way. Such a connection will never be lost.

When we come to faith in Christ, we are connected with our heavenly Father through Jesus Christ. This means that anytime we come before the Lord, He meets us there. We can have the confidence to go before Him with our needs and requests because we know He hears and answers us. This access point is a gift of grace, bought for us by the precious blood of Jesus. But like the merchants, we too can squander it. Our sinful tendencies cause us to pursue the desires of our flesh and worship our idols in God's place. But when we confess our sin and reorient our worship back to the Lord, He cleanses the idolatrous and selfish areas of our hearts by His grace. As we take our worship to the Lord seriously, He will remind us of the gift it is to have access to our heavenly Father. Our Savior has purchased this gift, so let us treasure it, coming before Him with grateful and worshipful hearts.

day thirty-three questions

How are you tempted to take your access to God lightly through prayer?

Jesus executed righteous anger over the desecration of worship to God. How should we respond when worship to God is belittled or desecrated?

Read Hebrews 10:19-23. How does the reminder of what Christ has accomplished for you encourage you in prayer?

DAY 34

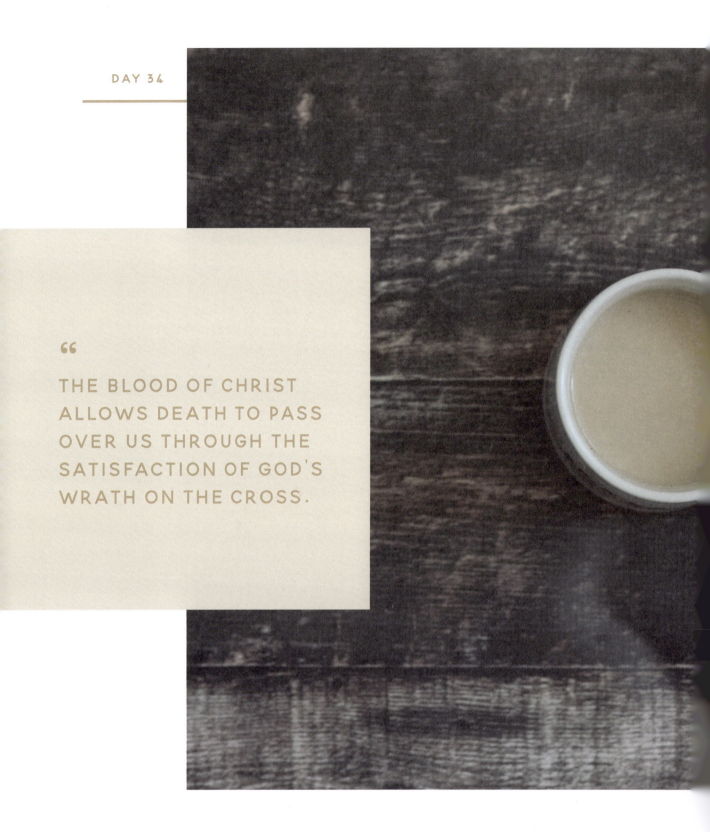

> THE BLOOD OF CHRIST ALLOWS DEATH TO PASS OVER US THROUGH THE SATISFACTION OF GOD'S WRATH ON THE CROSS.

Last Supper

READ MATTHEW 26:17-30, MARK 14:12-26, LUKE 22:7-38, JOHN 13:1-38

The week of Jesus's triumphant entry to His crucifixion and resurrection is now referred to as Holy Week. This week held substantial events during the time of Jesus. The recounting of that week gives a glimpse into what took place during Jesus's last few days. Christians, today, commemorate this week leading up to Easter Sunday, which serves as a celebration of Jesus's resurrection from the dead. Another event, among others, that took place during that week was the Passover meal shared among Jesus and His disciples. This meal took place the night before Jesus was arrested, put on trial, and sentenced to death—an event that provides a dramatic shift in the last few days of Jesus's life leading up to the cross. Today, this event is remembered year-round in what many churches refer to as the Lord's Supper, Communion, or the Lord's Table, in remembrance of what took place this very night.

The Passover was a Jewish tradition of holding a special meal to serve in remembrance of the Lord their God. This tradition was first established as a command by God to the Jews to have a Passover meal each year as a reminder of God saving them out of hundreds of years of slavery in Egypt (Exodus 12:21-27). In the act of freeing the Israelites, God brought about numerous plagues, including killing the firstborn sons in Egypt. However, God spared the firstborns of the Jews because Moses instructed them to kill a sacrificial lamb and sprinkle its blood over the doors so that death would pass over their homes. So this miraculous event was remembered yearly and referred to as the Passover.

When we come to Mark 14:12 in the New Testament, it is time for the Passover feast to take place. Jesus gives very detailed instructions about how to prepare the feast. He instructs the disciples to meet a man in the city, carrying a jug of water, and follow him to the next house he enters.

Jesus then tells them to find the owner of the house and ask about a large furnished room upstairs, where they will go to make preparations for the feast. The disciples did just that. When the time came, Jesus joined His disciples to eat and celebrate. But instead of light and jovial conversation, Jesus had a surprising message to deliver. Sitting among those who had followed Him closely and likely had become near and dear friends to Him, He shared that one of them would betray Him. It is difficult to fathom such a hurtful betrayal, which is why many of the disciples grew distressed, saying, "Surely not I!?" But Jesus insisted, "It is one of the Twelve—the one who is dipping bread in the bowl with me. For the Son of Man will go just as it is written about him, but woe to that man by whom the Son of Man is betrayed! It would have been better for him if he had not been born" (Mark 14:20-21).

Jesus followed up such accusations by continuing to eat with His disciples. Even with knowledge of such betrayal, He remained with them and ate. As they were eating, Jesus took the traditional elements of the Passover feast: unleavened bread and wine. He broke the bread and shared it with them, saying, "Take it; this is my body" (Mark 14:23). Then he took the cup of wine and shared it with them saying, "This is my blood of the covenant, which is poured out for many. Truly I tell you, I will no longer drink the fruit of the vine until that day when I drink it new in the kingdom of God" (Mark 14:24-25). Jesus was adding to this long-held tradition of looking back to God's faithfulness by pointing forward to His faithfulness enacted through His sacrificial death to come. A meal that had always pointed back to Exodus was now pointing to the cross of Christ. Jesus broke the bread and alluded that His body would be broken for them. He drank the cup of wine and alluded that His blood would be poured out for them. The disciples drank in remembrance of Him and concluded the meal by singing a hymn and then going out to the Mount of Olives.

Today, when churches observe Communion or the Lord's Supper, Christians are invited to partake in this meal. All who have put their hope and faith in the sacrificial death and redemptive resurrection of Jesus Christ are invited to remember the faithfulness of God through this observation. In doing so, we remember the extent to which God would go to save His people, not only from slavery in Egypt but from enslavement to the sin and death of this world. In the same way that the blood of the lamb allowed death to pass over the Jews in Egypt, so the blood of Christ allows death to pass over us through the satisfaction of God's wrath on the cross. As we drink and eat, we praise God in thankfulness for His faithfulness to His people, and we proclaim that the Lord will come again. And when He does, God will unite with His people, breaking the chains of our bondage to sin and death once and for all. He will gather us together, bringing His redemptive story full circle, and invite us to join Him at the Great Feast on the Last Day (Isaiah 25:6-10). May we, today, partake in this sacrament with great expectation and hope because of what God has done and will do.

> " **JESUS BROKE THE BREAD AND ALLUDED THAT HIS BODY WOULD BE BROKEN FOR THEM.**

day thirty-four questions

What is the Passover?

How did Jesus redefine the Passover meal?

Why is the Lord's Supper important for us to observe regularly?

Reflection

REVIEW ALL PASSAGES FROM THE LAST 6 DAYS

Summarize the main points from this week's Scripture readings.

What did you observe from this week's passages about the life of Jesus and His character?

What do this week's passages reveal about the condition of mankind and yourself?

How do these passages point to the gospel?

How should you respond to these Scriptures? What specific action steps can you take this week to apply them in your life?

Write a prayer in response to your study of God's Word. Adore God for who He is, confess sins He revealed in your own life, ask Him to empower you to walk in obedience, and pray for anyone who comes to mind as you study.

DAY 35

> IT IS IN OUR LOVE AND SERVICE FOR OTHERS, NO MATTER WHO THEY ARE OR WHAT THEY HAVE DONE, THAT THE WORLD WILL SEE THE LOVE OF CHRIST.

Jesus Washes the Disciples Feet

READ JOHN 13:1-17

As the Passover festivities are celebrated throughout Jerusalem, Jesus and His disciples gathered together to share the traditional meal and remember the Lord's work in the exodus from Egypt. Chapters 13-16 of John detail this celebration and the last words of Jesus to His disciples and all generations who will follow Him. These are extraordinary passages of Scripture, and they are known as some of the most comforting for believers to read.

At the time of this dinner, Jesus is only a few hours away from being arrested and put on trial. Though innocent, He will be found guilty and sentenced to death. Jesus will be the final Passover Lamb whose shed blood takes away the shame and guilt of all who believe in Him. He will give His people access to the Lord once more. This is the hour for which He has come. It is the purpose of His incarnation and the closing of His public ministry.

And in the last hours before His death, He chooses to be with His disciples to express His love for them. Before John even tells us of Jesus's profound act of service in this chapter, He reminds us that Jesus loved "to the end" those He had been given in His earthly ministry. This phrase means He loved the twelve disciples and all those who followed Him to "the fullest extent" or "to the uttermost." And this love was not only for them but for all who believe and follow Him until He returns once more. John shifts to take note of how, at the time of this supper, the devil was working in Judas Iscariot to betray Jesus. Judas was closely involved with the ministry of Jesus, observed His life and miracles, listened to His teaching, and still did not believe. Judas is the contrast to Jesus's life of humility. Judas would betray the disciples and Jesus, but Jesus would be with His friends until the end.

In the time Jesus lived and walked the earth, it was customary for homes to have a basin of water outside the door so that people could wash their feet before entering. Men and women wore sandals, if they wore shoes at all, and these sandals were no match for the dirt and filth of the streets and towns. If a household could afford servants, the lowest servant of them would be the one to wash the guests' feet before they dined. It was a humiliating job that no servant would want to do. However, it was necessary as guests ate reclined at tables. One's head may very well be next to other guests' feet during the meal, so most would have wanted their feet to be clean.

Luke 22 tells us that when the disciples gathered together with Jesus for the Passover meal, they were arguing about which of them was the greatest of His disciples. They did not understand the humility of Christ and the Messiah He was. However, they would soon witness the fullest form of His humiliation as He died an undeserved death on a Roman cross, an execution reserved for the worst of criminals. If any of them could have demanded honor and recognition that night, it was Jesus since these were the final moments before His great sacrifice. But Jesus, our humble Savior, does what the disciples would not consider doing for each other. He gets up from supper, lays aside His robe, takes a towel, pours water in a basin, and begins to wash each of the disciples' feet.

The disciples must have been taken back as their Savior took on the role of a servant on their behalf. Peter was aghast over Jesus's actions because Peter knew that Jesus was the Lord and that he was a sinful man. He believed that he should be the one to wash Jesus's feet. The disciple declared to Jesus to stop, but Jesus revealed to Peter the meaning behind what He was doing. If Jesus does not wash Peter's feet, Peter would not have any part of Jesus, so Peter quickly changes his mind and tells Jesus to wash all of him! You can hear Peter's desperation for closeness and intimacy with His Savior. Jesus tells Peter that he is already clean because he has already been washed. In those few words, Jesus gives Peter assurance of his salvation. Christ has fully washed Peter.

Jesus is showing Peter something that all believers would need to understand. To receive spiritual cleansing, we must be washed in the righteous blood of Jesus, but once that is done, we are saved and are free from the power of sin and death. We do not need to be cleansed again and again and again for salvation. However, as we live our lives on Earth, we will struggle with sin. When we come to Jesus in confession and for forgiveness, He renews us so that we become more like Him. In a sense, He does for us what He did for the disciples. He washes our feet and refreshes us with His presence and love.

Jesus told the disciples that they must follow His example. He washed their feet to show them they needed to be cleansed but also to show them that they must serve others out of love. For if their master and teacher chose to wash the feet of His students and followers, they must certainly do the same. Jesus poured out His tender love for these men, even in their quarreling over earthly status and authority. The love He displayed for them is also for us. Through John's account of Christ's last night before His death on the cross, we see the love by which He wants us to live. Like the disciples, we can be focused on this life and forget our eternal home with our Savior. It is in our love and service for others, no matter who they are or what they have done, that the world will see the love of Christ. And it is by walking in the love of Christ that we are transformed. He enables us to love because He has cleansed our hearts and washed us clean. Following His example will bring us the greatest joy.

day thirty-five questions

What do you learn about Jesus and His character by reading John 13:1-7?

Why is it significant that this is one of the final acts of Christ before His death on the cross?

How should you live in light of today's Scripture reading?

DAY 36

> IT IS KIND AND GRACIOUS OF OUR GOD TO GIVE US A CLEAR WAY TO KNOW HIM.

Jesus the Way, the Truth, and the Life

READ JOHN 14:1-14

After Jesus washes His disciples' feet, He shares with them words that may have brought alarm. Jesus lets them know that He will be leaving soon. The disciples ask where He is going. Jesus only replies that where He goes, they cannot come, but they will follow Him one day. We can only imagine how distressed the disciples likely were, in light of Jesus's words. The master they followed so closely was leaving them. What were they to do? As we open up chapter 14, Jesus seeks to bring comfort to the disciples in light of this news, telling them their hearts do not need to be troubled. All they needed to do at that moment was trust Him.

Jesus followed up His command to trust with the reason why they can trust Him. He did not plan to abandon them. Instead, where He was going was where they would live too. He was leaving, but He was going to prepare a place for them to join Him. In His house are many rooms, which means that this place will be available for as many who will believe. Jesus promises His disciples that He will prepare a place for them and come back to bring them to this place. At this point, the disciples are probably relieved but a little confused. Where is this place that Jesus is speaking about to them? And how do they get there? When Jesus tells His disciples that they already know how to get to this place, Thomas steps forward to ask the question that is likely on all the disciples' minds: "If we do not know where we are going, how do we know the way?" To the disciples, it probably felt like Jesus was setting them up for failure. It would be as if someone told you of an amazing place to go but failed to give you the location of it. There would be no knowing how to get there!

Jesus does not leave His disciples hanging but rather, provides the answer to Thomas's question: "I am the way" (John 14:6). Not only is He the way, but He is also the truth and the life. Jesus as the way is the main emphasis of this passage, but His mention of being the truth and the life is also significant. It is because Jesus is truth and life that He is also the way. To know Jesus is to know the truth that there is nothing else that can bring salvation but Him. To know Jesus is also to experience everlasting life from His salvation. By Jesus saying that He is the way, He was stating absolute exclusivity of salvation. There is no other way to get to heaven without believing in Him. He is the only way. By this statement, Jesus also claimed unity with the Father. Believers know Jesus because they belong to Him, and because they belong to Him, they have access to the Father.

Jesus tried to explain this to the disciples. By knowing Him, they knew God. By seeing Him, they saw God. But again, the disciples did not seem to understand. This time, Philip steps forward and asks Jesus to show them the Father. If they can see God, then they would believe. But the disciples have missed an essential part about being a disciple of Jesus. By being with Jesus, they have been with God. They do not need to be shown the Father; all they need to do is look at Jesus. To try to get them to understand this, Jesus explains His relationship to the Father, yet again. John 14:10-11 teaches us important elements to the doctrine of the Trinity. God, Jesus, and the Holy Spirit are one. Even though the Holy Spirit is not listed here, other passages of the gospels speak to this reality. Because Jesus is one with God, both He and God dwell within one another: God is in Jesus, and Jesus is in God. This is what Jesus means by "the Father dwells in me" and "I am in the Father and the Father is in me." This communicates the complete unity within the Godhead. Jesus and God are not independent of each other. Rather, they are two persons but one God. The disciples failed to understand this profound truth. The man they walked with was God in the flesh. Even if the disciples did not believe this, Jesus says they can believe based on the miracles He has shown them. These miracles should be enough proof that God is at work through Him, and in doing so, prove that Jesus is God.

But then Jesus adds another layer to belief in Him. John 14:6 reveals that belief in Him leads to God, but verse 12 goes on to say that whoever believes in Him will do even greater works than He did. This does not mean that believers will do more impressive miracles than Jesus. Jesus brought the dead to life, caused storms to cease, and multiplied loaves and fishes. Those who believe in Him will do great things but not anything beyond what Jesus has already done. Their works would be greater because their works would point to the finished work of Jesus on the cross. Not everyone believed Jesus's testimony about Himself even though He did miracles. But the disciples' works would testify to Jesus's death and resurrection. Through the Holy Spirit, His power within them would give them the ability to do great works for His glory.

Through Jesus, the disciples would do great works, but God would also answer their prayers. Jesus told them that whatever they asked in prayer, they would receive. This verse must be taken with caution, as it is often taken out of context to teach that whatever we ask in prayer will always be given a "yes" from God. If we look closely, we see two important aspects of this granted prayer: it involves praying prayers that are glorifying to God and are done in Jesus's name. To pray in Jesus's name is to ask something according to His will and who He is, something that reflects His character. To ask for something sinful or something apart from His sovereign will would not be praying in Jesus's name but rather our own. Prayers that glorify God are prayers that honor God and give Him praise. These are the prayers that Jesus promises to grant.

This passage teaches valuable truth that is necessary for us as believers. First, it teaches the unity of the Trinity. The relationship between the Father and Son demonstrates their relationship of complete unity. It is important that we see all three persons of the Trinity as one God. But the unity with Jesus and God is also a unity that is shared amongst believers. Two parts of this passage point to this unity, our place and prayers with God. For Jesus to prepare a place for believers and bring them to Himself shows God's desire to dwell with His people. Jesus did not come to Earth to abandon His people but save them and bring them to Himself. But our prayer with God also speaks to our unity with Him. Because of our relationship with Jesus, we have access to God in prayer. But our close connection with the Lord is what enables answered prayer. It is our unity with Him that brings about united prayers. As we remain connected to Jesus, desiring to glorify the Lord in all things, our will and His will unite in prayer. May we never think that our prayers are powerless, for the Lord uses the prayers of His people to accomplish His grand purposes.

Lastly, this passage emphasizes the exclusivity of salvation. Our world often teaches there are many ways to get to heaven, and all religions lead to God. But for Jesus to say that He is "the way the truth and the life" means that He is the one true way for salvation. Nothing else leads to a relationship with God apart from Jesus—not our good works, social standing, or skill set. This truth brings clarity and comfort. God has not left us wondering how we can get to Him. He has shown us the way, and it is through His Son. It is kind and gracious of our God to give us a clear way to know Him. Because Jesus is the way, we do not need to search for anything else beyond Him as a way to eternal life. It is through belief in Him alone that we have a relationship with our heavenly Father. What a comfort it is to have all that we need through Jesus Christ. In Him we find the way, absolute truth, and everlasting life.

> **"** IT IS BECAUSE JESUS IS TRUTH AND LIFE THAT HE IS ALSO THE WAY. TO KNOW JESUS IS TO KNOW THE TRUTH THAT THERE IS NOTHING ELSE THAT CAN BRING SALVATION BUT HIM.

> Jesus did not come to earth to abandon his people but save them and bring them to himself.

day thirty-six questions

Why is the exclusivity of salvation through Christ important to our evangelism? How can you use John 14:6 to speak truth to those who think there are multiple ways to get to heaven?

How does knowing Jesus is the way, the truth, and the life give you security in your salvation?

How should John 14:13-14 strengthen our prayer lives?
How does this challenge you in your prayers to God?

DAY 37

> THE LOVE OF GOD IS POWERFUL, AND WE CAN NEVER FATHOM ITS DEPTH.

Jesus the True Vine

READ JOHN 15:1-17

As Jesus prepared for the cross and His future departure, He prepared the hearts of His disciples by giving them words of encouragement. In John 15:1, Jesus gave His last "I am" statement: "I am the true vine." Here, Jesus illustrates the connection His followers have with Him. He is the vine, God is the vinedresser, and His followers are the branches.

From the very beginning, Jesus gave the purpose of being a branch: to bear fruit. As the vinedresser, God maintains the vine by pruning and removing branches. Those who do not bear fruit are removed, and those who do bear fruit are pruned to bear more fruit. As we look deeper into this illustration, we see it is the vine that declares who truly belongs to Jesus. A thriving vine is not a vine that has no fruit. In fact, a vine with no fruit would indicate a dead vine. But a living and thriving vine is a vine that has much fruit. This illustration makes a comparison between those who believe and follow Christ and those who do not. As the vine, Jesus is a life source. If someone has no evidence of fruit in his or her life or visible signs of a changed heart, that person most likely is not connected to the vine. Jesus's "I am" statement was not meant to alarm the disciples but to encourage them. As His followers, their faith in Him demonstrated that they belonged to Him. Through their time with Him, Jesus continually spoke words of truth that shaped and changed their hearts. This is why Jesus said that they are already clean. By the cleansing power of Jesus, they received life through Him. This is what secured them as branches on the vine.

Jesus not only gave them encouragement that they belonged to Him but challenged them to continue clinging to Him. The word "abide" means "to remain." What Jesus was not saying through this command was that they better hang on to Him or they would be let go from the vine. Because they belong to Jesus, there is no possibility of them being removed from the vine. Rather, Jesus was saying to continue in their fellowship with Him. Being part of the vine meant that the disciples were united to Christ. He was in them, and they were in Him. This is an intimate and strong connection. In light of Jesus's departure, He encouraged the disciples to take advantage of their everlasting connection with Him. A branch cannot be dependent on anything else for its source of life apart from the vine. In the same way, it was only by depending on Christ that they had life and the power to bear fruit. Jesus added on to the consequence of those who do not bear fruit by saying those branches will be cast in the fire. This depicts the reality of those who choose not to follow Christ. Without life in Him, they are cast away to experience the punishment of death. Again, Jesus does not tell the disciples this truth to scare them into obedience. Jesus is pointing out that many Jews have said they follow God, but they show no fruit as evidence. They believed they belonged to the vine because of their Jewish heritage, but their lack of fruit showed that they did not know Jesus. As the disciples navigated their ministry, they would be able to discern true followers of Christ by examining their fruit and warning those who thought they belonged to the vine to believe in Jesus.

Jesus added another layer to the outcome of abiding: abiding in Christ results in glorifying God. The fruit the disciple bore would bring glory to God. Jesus highlighted one fruit of abiding love. Jesus told the disciples they had a love of God. The same love between God and Jesus is the same love between Jesus and His followers. This is incredible! The love of God is powerful, and we can never fathom its depth. To receive this abundant love is a gift. Second, Jesus said that it is out of this great love that the disciples were to be obedient. Bearing fruit was meant to be a delight for the disciples, not a duty. It was out of love from God and for God that the disciples were to obey Christ's commandments. This is what separated the disciples from other religious Jews. It was out of an obligation to keep rules that motivated the obedience of many Jews. In contrast, it was out of a response of love for the Lord that motivated the disciples' obedience. Delighting in Christ and His love for His followers is what encourages obedience. By this command, Jesus taught them how they should bear fruit: By being obedient to Him! As the disciples followed His commands, they would bear fruit in their lives.

However, the disciples' love was not to be kept only between themselves and God but extended to others. And Jesus shows them what it looks like to love others. In John 15:13, Jesus said that there is no greater love than laying down one's life for his friends. Jesus would demonstrate this great love by laying down His life and dying on the cross. Jesus's sacrificial love is an example of the sacrificial love that we should extend to others. We may not physically lay down our life for another, but we can reflect Christ's sacrificial love by laying down our desires for the sake of others.

Lastly, Jesus connects the disciples' abiding with prayer. Just as in John 14, He told the disciples that if they abide in Him, they could ask anything in prayer, and it would be granted. Again, this granted prayer is connected to the relationship Jesus had with His followers. Like John 14, there are two conditions for this answered prayer: abiding in Jesus and His words abiding in us. As we abide in Christ by remaining dependent on Him and dwelling on His words given to us through Scripture, we will come to desire what He desires. As we do so, we come to pray prayers that are in accordance with Christ's will.

All of these words Jesus spoke to the disciples were to give them complete and lasting joy. They did not need to worry that their connection with Christ would be lost after His departure. Because they belonged to Him, they belonged to the vine, and therefore they had a reason to rejoice. As believers in Christ, we, too, have the fullness of joy by our connection with the vine. Just like the disciples, we receive the blessings of the love of God, the power of Christ, and the joy of the Lord in our connection with Jesus. Jesus's exhortation to the disciples to abide in Him is His same exhortation to us. Our connection with God through Christ is a gift of grace. We should not take this connection lightly by choosing to depend on ourselves apart from the vine. Jesus is our source of life, so seeking anything else apart from Him hinders our ability to bear fruit and leads to spiritual dryness. Apart from Him, we cannot do anything, so for us to bear fruit, we must abandon self-sufficiency. But as we bear fruit, we must do so as an act of delight for Him and not out of duty. If we misread this passage, we can think that God's love and the security of salvation are contingent on our obedience. But the gospel is good news because Christ's obedience saves us. Through our salvation with Christ, we are secured to the vine forever, even if we struggle to bear fruit. This frees us to bear fruit out of a response to the love of Christ. It is an honor to be chosen and appointed by God to bear fruit for Him. Let us be faithful branches on the vine and delight in bearing fruit for our great God.

day thirty-seven questions

Read Hebrews 12:5-11. How does seeing God's pruning as something done for our good change the way you view His pruning? What are some things you need to allow Him to prune so you can be fruitful?

What is the difference between being Christ's friend and His servant? How does this impact the way you see your relationship with Him?

Read Galatians 5:22-23. How do you see this fruit apparent in your life?

DAY 38

> JESUS'S FINAL HOPE AND PRAYER IS THAT GOD WOULD FULFILL HIS PROMISE TO HIS PEOPLE THROUGH HIM.

Jesus's High Priestly Prayer

READ JOHN 17

This study refers often to Jesus as our great High Priest. This is one of His primary roles to us, which is clarified and explained in Hebrews 4:14-15: "Therefore, since we have a great high priest who has passed through the heavens—Jesus the Son of God—let us hold fast to our confession. For we do not have a high priest who is unable to sympathize with our weaknesses, but one who has been tempted in every way as we are, yet without sin." In the Old Testament, the high priest was a spiritual leader for God's people. Their role was to intercede between God and His people, making sacrifices on behalf of their sins as a means of atonement. However, every earthly priest of Scripture was limited and could never fully bear the weight of the people's sins by making sacrifices day in and day out. They could never accomplish a once and for all atonement and were merely shadows of the true high priest to come in Jesus Christ. So as we enter into John 17, we witness Jesus stepping into this role as our great High Priest, interceding in prayer on our behalf and ultimately following the will of God the Father to make atonement for our sins once and for all through His sacrificial death. This is why this prayer is referred to as Jesus's High Priestly Prayer.

In the same way, prayer reveals a person's heart, so this prayer gives us a glimpse into the heart and mind of Jesus in His final moments. The prayer recorded in this chapter exudes grief, submission, and hope all the same. Finding Himself in the garden of Gethsemane, Jesus knew the cross was before Him. He knew He was awaiting His death. And yet, He knew the will of the Father and the hope that would come from submitting to it. Therefore when the time came, He went to be alone to spend time in personal communion with the Father—lifting His eyes, pleading to Him, acknowledging Him, honoring Him, and making requests.

Jesus's prayer was ultimately categorized into three portions: a prayer for Himself, a prayer for His disciples, and a prayer for all believers. His beginning request was glorification, which means receiving the highest degree of praise and honor. But it was not simply for His glory. Instead, He asked to be glorified so that the Father would be glorified through Him (John 17:1). His ultimate aim was to exalt the Father. It was only secondary that He requested the glory due to His name. Jesus set aside His glory when He came to the world as a man (Philippians 2:5-8). He was still perfectly God and perfectly human but humbled Himself, not to count Himself equal with God. Jesus requested that God reunite Jesus to Himself and for God to return His glory to Him when the work on the cross was accomplished. God granted this request when, "...God highly exalted him and gave him the name that is above every name, so that at the name of Jesus every knee will bow—in heaven and on earth and under the earth—and every tongue will confess that Jesus Christ is Lord, to the glory of God the Father" (Philippians 2:9-11).

Following these requests, Jesus interceded for His disciples. He walked so closely with these men and likely considered them His greatest earthly friendships. He shared His heart and ministry with them, teaching them the Scriptures and entrusting them with the great hope of the gospel. Jesus knew His disciples would be the ones to carry forth the good news of salvation brought by His death and resurrection. So, He offered up specific requests to the Father to be implemented once He left this world. He asked God to protect them. Not only did He ask that they be protected from the persecution of the world that hated them for bringing such a message, but He asked that they be protected spiritually from the evil one by remaining in Him. This "remaining" Jesus spoke of was enacted with His physical presence while He walked with them but would be enacted with His eternal presence through salvation on the other side of the cross—just as He said in His final earthly words to His disciples, "And remember, I am with you always, to the end of the age" (Matthew 28:20b). Lastly, He asked for them to be continually sanctified by truth and sustained with joy through their ministry. He was essentially asking God to bring fruit from the Words He imparted to them, that they would remain faithful and hopeful to the end.

In the last portion of His prayer, Jesus oriented His heart to pray for all believers. In the same way, He imparted the truth of the gospel to His disciples; He prayed for the truth of the gospel to go forth, bringing people to know Him as their Lord and Savior. He focused primarily on uniting believers under the banner of His name and prayed that this truth would serve as a foundation for unity among His people. With so many differences among social, cultural, racial, educational, and political lines, people can easily cultivate division and hostility. But unity is found through salvation in Jesus Christ. And that unity not only serves as a witness to a watching world but also serves as a glimpse of our eternal union with God. This is precisely what Jesus came to accomplish through His life, death, and resurrection. Jesus's final hope and prayer is that God would fulfill His promise to His people through Him, binding them together in unity and bringing them to glory in Him.

day thirty-eight questions

What stands out to you about this prayer?
What do you learn about the character of Jesus by reading it?

How is Jesus more concerned with God's glory over His own?
How can we exemplify this in our own lives?

Jesus prays for believers to be united under the banner of His name as both a witness to non-believers and as an encouragement to believers. How have you witnessed unity in the gospel accomplishing these things?

DAY 39

> "
> JESUS DRANK FROM THE CUP OF WRATH SO THAT WE COULD DRINK FROM THE CUP OF SALVATION.

Arrest at Gethsemane

READ MARK 14:32-50, JOHN 18:1-12

In the garden of Gethsemane, Jesus awaited His arrest. Jesus's heart ached with suffering as He knew He had to face the Lord's wrath for sin. When He prayed to the Father there, He referenced Old Testament symbolism. The symbol of God's cup of wrath signified His judgment upon the wicked. The prophet Isaiah spoke of this imagery when he warned the Israelites about the impending doom that would fall on their kingdom if they continued to disobey God. Isaiah said, "Wake yourself, wake yourself up! Stand up, Jerusalem, you who have drunk the cup of his fury from the Lord's hand; you who have drunk the goblet to the dregs—the cup that causes people to stagger" (Isaiah 51:17). Drinking the bitter contents of the cup, or experiencing the Lord's righteous anger, would cause people to fall into destruction for their sin. But Jesus would remove this cup of wrath from God's people by taking it on Himself. God's people would never again drink from the cup of wrath (Isaiah 51:22) because Jesus would drink the contents to the last sip and walk willingly into the hands of the arresting authorities.

During the night, Jesus went to the garden of Gethsemane on the Mount of Olives. This location was significant as Scripture notes both gardens and mountains as places of deep intimacy with God. Jesus brought Peter, James, and John—the men who saw the transfiguration (Matthew 17:1-8), which confirmed Jesus's death was a part of His heavenly mission. When they arrived, Jesus said He was deeply troubled. Because such sorrow and grief overwhelmed Him, Jesus was moved to pray and urged the disciples to pray with Him. When alone, Jesus called out, "Abba, Father! All things are possible for you. Take this cup away from me" (Mark 14:36a). Like a child calling out for help, Jesus cried out to His Father and asked if God could do anything to remove His cup of wrath. In Matthew's account, Jesus presented this request three times. But, always in the very next sentence, Jesus submitted to the plan of salvation devised before the foundation of the world. In humility, He stated, "Nevertheless, not what I will, but what you will" (Mark 14:36b). When Jesus returned to His disciples, they were asleep. Like the prophet Isaiah calling the Israelites to wake in Isaiah 51:17, Jesus called the disciples to wake up and witness the cup of wrath through His attackers approaching in the distance.

Judas, one of the twelve disciples, came with a mob of soldiers sent from the chief priests and elders. Judas was paid to lead them there so that Jesus could be arrested for blasphemy and later executed. The mob came with weapons like Jesus was a violent rebel, but Jesus would not resist the arrest because no one would take His life forcibly. As the God-Man, Jesus was the only One able to give up His life willingly as the sacrifice for His people. Marking Jesus as the one to capture, Judas greeted Him with a kiss on the cheek. This sign typically conveyed respect and warmth, but here, it dripped instead with greed and deceit. Jesus called Judas "friend" (Matthew 26:50), proving Judas to be the great betrayer. However, Judas did not have to mark Him—Jesus openly declared He was the One they were looking for (John 18:5). Scholars point out that in the "I am he" statement, Jesus did not hide; He was no victim but the orchestrator of His arrest. But, Peter still responded in defense and cut off an officer's ear. Peter again misunderstood that Jesus's arrest and death was the will of God so that prophecies like Zechariah 13:7 would be fulfilled. Jesus healed the man's ear, showing Peter that His ministry would now bring redemption through His suffering and humiliation. After this gracious act, Jesus was chained.

Jesus drank from the cup of wrath so that we could drink from the cup of salvation (Psalm 116:13). He drank the fullness of its bitter contents so that we could taste the sweet love and forgiveness of God. He agonized in Gethsemane so that we could have peace and rest in the garden. Jesus bound Himself in sin and judgment and was taken to the court of God on our behalf. Because of His saving work, we are freed from guilt and can have an intimate relationship with the Father. But, we will still grieve over the fallen world full of injustice, hatred, and greed. We will still wrestle over the persistent sin in our hearts. Nevertheless, let us not be like the disciples whose grief and distress led them to sleep (Luke 22:45). In other words, let us not check out when circumstances are hard and darkness is all around. We can pray to remain vigilant against our flesh and the schemes of Satan. Let us be watchful so that we do not fall into temptation. The hour of the Lord's second coming will arrive when Jesus, who was arrested for the unjust, will arrest all evil and restore God's kingdom completely.

> " HE DRANK THE FULLNESS OF ITS BITTER CONTENTS SO THAT WE COULD TASTE THE SWEET LOVE AND FORGIVENESS OF GOD.

day thirty-nine questions

In what ways does Jesus's prayer in the garden of Gethsemane display both His divine and human natures?

How has your flesh been weak against fighting temptation?

Write out a prayer asking for strength to stay near the cross, no matter your circumstances.

DAY 40

> JESUS'S DEATH AND BURIAL WERE NOT THE END BUT ONLY THE BEGINNING.

Crucifixion and Burial

READ MATTHEW 27:27-66

The time finally arrived for Jesus to accomplish what He came to do. From the beginning of His life on earth, Jesus took a posture of humility, and now at the end of His earthly life, He would fully display His humility. It is very easy for us to want to skip over the nature and details of Jesus's death or quickly read through verses like those for today's reading. But to understand the glorious good news of the gospel, we must sit with the heavy reality of what Jesus endured on the cross. The burden Jesus carried on this fateful day was both physical and spiritual. Physically, He would endure some of the most excruciating forms of torture that have ever been practiced. Spiritually, He would become all of the sins of God's people and thus be forced to drink the cup of God's wrath. We sing and talk about the cross often in Christian culture, but let us not gloss over the death of Christ.

After Jesus was given over to the Roman guard by Pilate at the urging of the Jewish people, He was flogged and beaten. It was customary for flogging to take place before every Roman execution. As the guards carried out the flogging, the blows would lessen as the criminal confessed his crimes, but since Jesus had no crimes to confess, all of His blows were probably strong and severe. After the flogging, the soldiers dress Jesus in a scarlet robe and place a crown of thorns on His head. Scarlet was the color of royalty. As they call out, "Hail, King of the Jews," they do not know that they are standing before the King of the universe, their very Creator. When they are done with their mockery, they strip Jesus of the scarlet robe. This would have been very painful for Him since His back would have been dripping with blood, and the blood would have begun to dry and clot on the robe. They reopen His wounds and lead Him to His crucifixion.

The Romans did not originally develop crucifixion, but they made it as torturous as possible. It was a form of death reserved for the worst of all criminals and the lowest social classes. A Roman citizen would have to commit a serious crime to be put to death this way. And yet, Jesus, God in flesh, willingly takes on the worst of all human deaths, knowing the end of what it will accomplish. As He is lifted on the cross, completely naked, bleeding, and battered, the worst part of His suffering takes place. He is separated from His heavenly Father. The Roman guards, passing spectators, religious leaders, and even other criminals hanging next to Him mock Him as He hangs on the cross. Yet before we look at them in anger and indignation, we must remember that we have done the same thing. The mockery and hatred toward Christ displayed in this passage reveal the condition of every human heart before God intervened on our behalf. We are opposed to the Lord, and we rebel against His authority as our King and Creator. We hate the One who made us, and yet He chooses to give us new hearts, allows us to repent, and restores us to Himself.

When we follow Christ, He calls us to the cross. Matthew 16:24 tells us to pick up our crosses and follow Him. In light of His suffering and what the cross was known for when He walked the earth, when Jesus calls us to pick up our crosses, He is calling us to life familiar with suffering, humiliation, and rejection from the world. Realizing the depth of His suffering and sacrifice for sin should also cause us not to take the sin in our own lives lightly.

As Jesus's death approached, a darkness came over the land in the middle of the afternoon. He calls out to the Lord and asks why His Father has forsaken Him. In doing this, He quotes the beginning words from Psalm 22, fulfilling another messianic prophecy. After being on the cross for six hours, Jesus gives another cry. Scripture tells us He cried with a loud voice, and then Jesus gave up His Spirit. No one took the life of Christ; He gave it willingly and joyfully to serve His Father and save His people. And as the Father accepts Jesus's sacrifice, the Father responds by tearing the temple curtain in two. The temple would have been filled with people at this time because they were celebrating Passover, and when the curtain ripped, they would have seen what no group of people had seen for hundreds of years: the Holy of Holies. Jesus's sacrifice obliterated the sacrificial system and need for the temple.

When Jesus died, the earth also started to quake, and rocks broke open. All of these events filled the people present at the crucifixion site with terror. Roman guards, who had just been taunting Jesus, said that He was truly the Son of God (Matthew 27:54). Jesus's body was taken down and buried in the family tomb of a rich man named Joseph. Joseph dressed Jesus's body for burial with Mary Magdalene and Jesus's mother present and closed the entrance of the tomb with a great stone.

The following day, the chief priests and Pharisees went to Pilate and asked him to provide strong security for the tomb of Christ. They claimed that Christ's disciples might come and steal His body and tell people that Jesus had fulfilled what He promised to do — to rise from the dead. However, after all they have witnessed, from the dark eclipse to the earth-shaking and the temple's curtain ripping from top to bottom, it appears that they are nervous. And so they should be because no torture or crucifixion could withhold the Son of God from overcoming the power of death. Jesus's death and burial were not the end but only the beginning.

day forty questions

Read Isaiah 53. What in the Old Testament prophecy reminds you of the account of Jesus's suffering and death in Matthew 27?

How do you tend to take sin lightly? How does reading this passage encourage you to react differently to sin in your life?

Write a prayer of awe and adoration for your Savior. Thank Him for His suffering, and ask Him to help you take up your cross and follow Him.

DAY 41

> " OUR PAIN AND TEARS MAY LINGER, BUT THEY ARE NOT ETERNAL IN LIGHT OF THE RESURRECTION.

Resurrection and Ascension

READ MATTHEW 28:1-20, MARK 16:1-20, LUKE 24:1-53, JOHN 20:1-21:25

Many good stories use the literary device of foreshadowing. An author will signal coming events to the reader and prepare them for plot twists. Similarly, throughout the Bible, God used foreshadowing to tell about His Son. By sending prophets and prophecies, He left clues that foretold details about Jesus's life, death, and resurrection. Jesus even told His disciples explicitly what would happen to Him—that He would be killed, buried, and rise again (Mark 9:30-32). But despite these clues, the people still did not understand Jesus's death. When Jesus was killed on a cross that dark, grievous Friday, His followers mourned and grieved. They were confused, afraid, and overwhelmed. It is in the midst of this darkness that we come to Resurrection Sunday.

Several days after Jesus's death, Mary, the mother of Jesus, and Mary Magdalene went to the tomb to anoint Jesus's body with oils. It was early on a Sunday, and the women were mourning the death of their friend and Savior. They would have expected to see a heavy stone rolled in front of the grave, but what they saw stopped them in their tracks. Instead of a large rock blocking the grave, they found the tomb open and an angel appeared to them. The angel was glorious and powerful and had an appearance that resembled lightning. When the women saw the angel, they were afraid.

The angel was compassionate and understood the women's reeling emotions—from grief to confusion to fear. The first words the angel spoke to these frightened women were, "Don't be afraid." He comforted them, even before delivering them the most remarkable news: "He is not here. For he is risen" (Matthew 28:6). The angel then spoke to the women about Jesus's resurrection and reminded the women of His words. They were amazed, perplexed, and confused. They were joyful but still terrified and unsure. They were so afraid, in fact, that they did not tell anyone right away (Mark 16:8). Ironically, just as the disciples fled in fear during Jesus's crucifixion, the women fled from His resurrection site. They could not fully comprehend that Jesus was alive!

Sometimes we can grow numb to how incredible the resurrection story is. If we have grown up in the church, we get used to hearing that Jesus rose from the dead. But consider afresh the power of this story today. Jesus, who is fully man and fully God, died a gruesome death on a cross. No one expected Him to rise from the dead that following Sunday. The religious leaders and the crowds wanted Him dead, and there was even concern about the safety of the disciples because of Friday's crucifixion. Many of the disciples hid in a locked room after Jesus's death out of fear of the Jews. But unlike every man killed before Him, Jesus's body did not sit and decay in a closed tomb. He rose from the dead, later appearing to the women, the disciples, and over 500 witnesses. He then ascended into heaven, where He now sits at the right hand of the Father. What an amazing miracle!

This resurrection is the foundation of our faith. It is what gives us hope and assurance. We do not need to be afraid because Jesus rose from the grave. Because of the resurrection, we have confidence that our sins are forgiven. Jesus not only paid the penalty of our sins on the cross, but He also rose from the dead to offer us new life.

Not only this, but we know that God is with us in all of life's trials—as we read in Romans 8:32, "He did not even spare his own Son but offered him up for us all. How will he not also with him grant us everything?" If God secured our greatest need through Christ's death and resurrection, how can we assume He will be absent in the day-to-day? Our pain and tears may linger, but they are not eternal in light of the resurrection. Our suffering may last for the night, but joy comes in the morning. One day we will be reunited with Christ, and all things will be made new. Even death will not be the end of our story because Jesus has removed the sting of death (1 Corinthians 15:55).

Just as the resurrection was foretold in the Bible, so is our future in eternity. One day, God will return to make all things right. He will wipe every tear and right every wrong (Revelation 21:4). The whole world will stand before Him, either covered by the blood of the Lamb and welcomed into His eternal kingdom or cast eternally from His presence. This truth should increase our urgency to share the gospel with others. The only way to be saved is by trusting in Jesus's perfect life, death and resurrection, and we have the great privilege of sharing this message with others (Matthew 28:18-20). It is a joyous commission because God has changed our lives forever. He has redeemed us and given us peace with God. He sustains us, helps us, loves us, and lives within us. He is worthy.

We serve a risen King. He is the living Christ, who has authority, dominion, and power over all things. He fulfills the prophecies of old. He is the true and better Adam, Moses, and David, and the Great High Priest. He is Emmanuel, Master, and Lord of lords. He has defeated the grave, and He is alive! Praise God, our King is alive!

day forty-one questions

How does the truth of the resurrection change your day-to-day life?

Read 1 Corinthians 15. How does Paul describe the significance of the resurrection?

Write a prayer of adoration in light of Christ's resurrection.
Thank Him for His sacrifice on the cross and for the power to overcome the grave.

The Number 40

THEMES IN SCRIPTURE

Just as we consider Lent for 40 days leading up to Easter, so we can see the theme of 40 days (or the number 40) in other parts of Scripture as well. We find periods of 40 days in Noah's story, in the Israelites wilderness wandering (though in that case, it is 40 years), when Moses receives the Law from God at Mount Sinai, and when Elijah flees Queen Jezebel. And there are indeed additional appearances of the number 40 found throughout Scripture.

THE FLOOD

Genesis 6:13-8:22

The severe wickedness of man causes the Lord to create a great flood on the earth. God does not punish everyone and everything, for He spares a righteous man named Noah and his family. God commissions Noah to build an ark and bring on it two of every kind of animal. Once built, Noah, his family, and the animals go onto the ark. God brings the flood, but Noah and his family are safe upon the ark. God's flood lasted 40 days and 40 nights. Once these days pass, the floodwaters cease, and Noah and his family come back to a restored earth. God also makes a covenant with Noah that He will never again destroy the earth in this way. These 40 days and 40 nights represent a period of hardship. However, God does not allow this hardship to last, for He brings the world back to a place of restoration.

ISRAEL IN THE WILDERNESS

Numbers 32:13, Joshua 5:6

After their exodus from Egypt, God leads the Israelites to the Promised Land. However, before coming to this land, God causes the Israelities to spend time in the wilderness. God uses these years to refine the Israelites, so they learn to depend on Him. Coming out of slavery in Egypt, the Israelites have to trust the Lord in difficult circumstances. Would they trust that He will take care of them? Sadly, the Israelites doubt the provision of the Lord and rebel against Him. As a punishment, God sends the Israelites into the wilderness for another 40 years. After the first generation of Israelites dies in the wilderness, God remains faithful to His covenant by taking the second generation to the Promised Land.

MOSES AT MOUNT SINAI

Exodus 24:18

After Moses receives the Ten Commandments, God makes a covenant with Moses at Mount Sinai. God commands Moses to stay on Mount Sinai, and Moses remains on the mountain for 40 days and 40 nights, receiving the Law from the Lord. These days in the Lord's presence are a time of preparation used to equip Moses for his leadership over Israel.

ELIJAH IN THE WILDERNESS

1 Kings 19:1-8

When Queen Jezebel threatens Elijah's life, Elijah flees to the wilderness to hide. Instead of leaving Elijah to die, the Lord sends an angel to give him food and water to sustain him. After being filled, Elijah fasts for 40 days and 40 nights before coming to Mount Horeb. At Mount Horeb, God comes to Elijah and gives him instruction on how to lead the nation of Israel during their rebellion.

Messianic Prophecies

OF THE OLD TESTAMENT FULFILLED IN JESUS CHRIST

MATTHEW 1:22-23 LUKE 1:31-35	The prophecy of the virgin birth and the naming of her son, Immanuel, in Isaiah 7:14 is fulfilled through the virgin birth of Mary and Jesus being Immanuel, God with us.
MATTHEW 2:5-6	Christ's birth in Bethlehem of Judah fulfills the prophecy in Micah 5:2, which says a ruler will come from Bethlehem in the land of Judah to save the people of Israel.
MATTHEW 2:14-15	The angel's command to Joseph to take Jesus from Bethlehem and flee to Egypt fulfills the prophecy of Hosea 11:1, which says, "out of Egypt I called my son."
MATTHEW 2:23	Jesus's home of Nazareth is the fulfillment of a theme of the prophets, which said that the coming Messiah would be despised. Nazareth was looked down upon by many people, so Jesus being a Nazarene caused Him to be despised.
MATTHEW 3:1-3 MARK 1:1-4 LUKE 3:4-6	John the Baptist's role in preparing the way for Jesus's ministry fulfills the prophecy of Isaiah 40:3 and Malachi 3:1, which prophesies a man in the wilderness who prepares the way of the Lord.
MATTHEW 4:13-16	Christ leaving Nazareth and living in Capernaum, the area of Zebulun and Naphtali, fulfills Isaiah 9:1-2 and Isaiah 42:7, which prophesies how the Messiah would bring light to the people in darkness from that specific region.
MATTHEW 12:15-21	Jesus's healings fulfill the prophecy of Isaiah 42:1-4, which prophesies the Messiah, whose mission is to restore and bring justice to the nations.

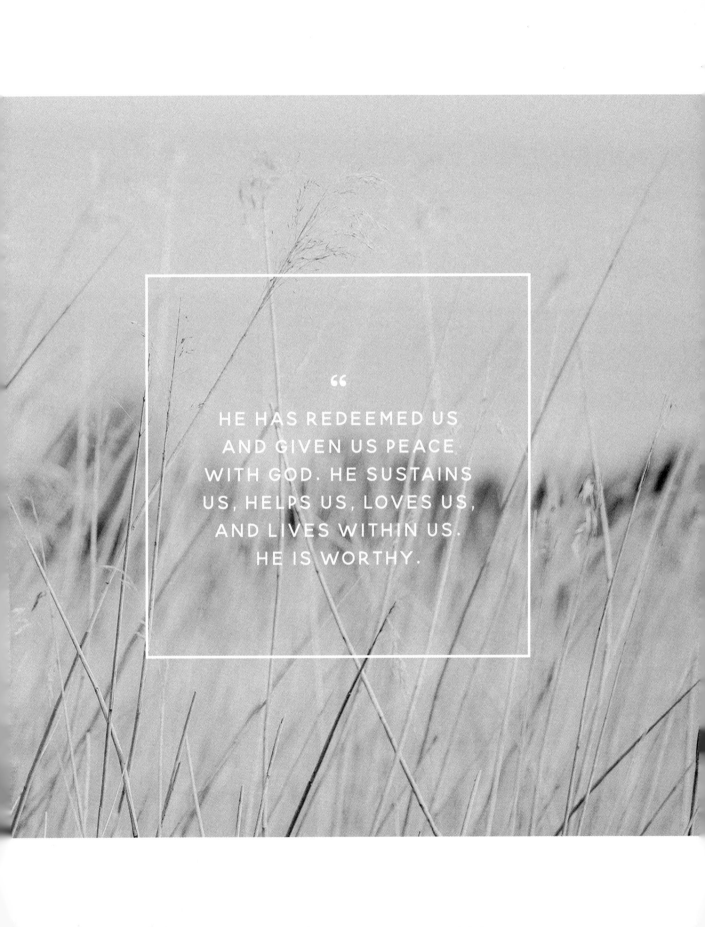

What is the Gospel?

THANK YOU FOR READING AND ENJOYING THIS STUDY WITH US! WE ARE ABUNDANTLY GRATEFUL FOR THE WORD OF GOD, THE INSTRUCTION WE GLEAN FROM IT, AND THE EVER-GROWING UNDERSTANDING IT PROVIDES FOR US OF GOD'S CHARACTER. WE ARE ALSO THANKFUL THAT SCRIPTURE CONTINUALLY POINTS TO ONE THING IN INNUMERABLE WAYS: THE GOSPEL.

We remember our brokenness when we read about the fall of Adam and Eve in the garden of Eden (Genesis 3), where sin entered into a perfect world and maimed it. We remember the necessity that something innocent must die to pay for our sin when we read about the atoning sacrifices in the Old Testament. We read that we have all sinned and fallen short of the glory of God (Romans 3:23) and that the penalty for our brokenness, the wages of our sin, is death (Romans 6:23). We all need grace and mercy, but most importantly, we all need a Savior.

We consider the goodness of God when we realize that He did not plan to leave us in this dire state. We see His promise to buy us back from the clutches of sin and death in Genesis 3:15. And we see that promise accomplished with Jesus Christ on the cross. Jesus Christ knew no sin yet became sin so that we might become righteous through His sacrifice (2 Corinthians 5:21). Jesus was tempted in every way that we are and lived sinlessly. He was reviled yet still yielded Himself for our sake, that we may have life abundant in Him. Jesus lived the perfect life that we could not live and died the death that we deserved.

The gospel is profound yet simple. There are many mysteries in it that we will never understand this side of heaven, but there is still overwhelming weight to its implications in this life. The gospel tells of our sinfulness and God's goodness and a gracious gift that compels a response. We are saved by grace through faith, which means that we rest with faith in the grace that Jesus Christ displayed on the cross (Ephesians 2:8-9). We cannot save ourselves from our brokenness or do any amount of good works to merit God's favor. Still, we can have faith that what Jesus accomplished in His death, burial, and resurrection was more than enough for our salvation and our eternal delight. When we accept God, we are commanded to die to ourselves and our sinful desires and live a life worthy of the calling we have received (Ephesians 4:1). The gospel compels us to be sanctified, and in so doing, we are conformed to the likeness of Christ Himself. This is hope. This is redemption. This is the gospel.

SCRIPTURES TO REFERENCE:

GENESIS 3:15 — *I will put hostility between you and the woman, and between your offspring and her offspring. He will strike your head, and you will strike his heel.*

ROMANS 3:23 — *For all have sinned and fall short of the glory of God.*

ROMANS 6:23 — *For the wages of sin is death, but the gift of God is eternal life in Christ Jesus our Lord.*

2 CORINTHIANS 5:21 — *He made the one who did not know sin to be sin for us, so that in him we might become the righteousness of God.*

EPHESIANS 2:8-9 — *For you are saved by grace through faith, and this is not from yourselves; it is God's gift — not from works, so that no one can boast.*

EPHESIANS 4:1-13 — *Therefore I, the prisoner in the Lord, urge you to walk worthy of the calling you have received, with all humility and gentleness, with patience, bearing with one another in love, making every effort to keep the unity of the Spirit through the bond of peace.*

*Thank you for studying
God's Word with us!*

CONNECT WITH US
@thedailygraceco
@dailygracepodcast

CONTACT US
info@thedailygraceco.com

SHARE
#thedailygraceco

VISIT US ONLINE
www.thedailygraceco.com

MORE DAILY GRACE
Daily Grace® Podcast